The Neuroscience of Connection: Brain Based Strategies for Love, Work, and Flourishing

Azhar ul Haque Sario

Copyright

First Printing, 2025

Azhar.sario@hotmail.co.uk

ORCID: https://orcid.org/0009-0004-8629-830X
Disclaimer: This book is free from AI use. The cover was designed in Microsoft Publisher

Contents

The Cognitive Cost of Connection: Reclaiming Focus in a Digital World

Okay, let's reimagine that content with a human touch, a unique angle, and a splash of creativity:

The Day My Brain Broke Up With My Phone
It started subtly. A forgotten birthday. A missed deadline. A conversation with my partner where my eyes glazed over, not because they were boring, but because my brain was halfway down a Twitter rabbit hole. Something was off. My once-sharp mind felt like a cluttered attic, thoughts scattered like dust bunnies in the corners.

Then, it hit me. My brain was staging a coup. It was tired of playing second fiddle to the glowing rectangle in my hand. Tired of the constant interruptions, the shallow dives into a million different topics, the dopamine hits that left me craving more, more, more.

See, our brains are wired for focus. For deep dives into complex ideas, for losing ourselves in the flow of a single task. But our phones, those seductive little devils, have other plans. They thrive on distraction, on fragmenting our attention into a thousand tiny pieces.

Imagine your brain as a magnificent orchestra, each section playing in harmony to create a beautiful symphony of thought. Now picture someone running through the orchestra, banging cymbals, tooting kazoos, and shouting random phrases. That's what our phones do to our poor, beleaguered brains.

And the worst part? We've become addicted to the chaos. Every notification is a tiny gamble, a chance to win the dopamine jackpot. We scroll and scroll, not because we're genuinely interested, but because our brains are hooked on the unpredictable rewards.

But here's the good news: we can break free. We can retrain our brains, strengthen our focus, and reclaim our cognitive sovereignty. It starts with small steps:

Declare "No Phone Zones": Create sacred spaces where your phone is banished – the dinner table, the bedroom, that cozy reading nook.
Embrace Boredom: Resist the urge to fill every quiet moment with your phone. Let your mind wander, daydream, and make unexpected connections.
Become a Mono-tasker: Our brains aren't designed to multitask. Focus on one thing at a time and savor the satisfaction of a job well done.
Digital Detox Dates: Schedule regular phone-free time. Go for a walk in nature, have a deep conversation with a friend, or simply lose yourself in a good book.
It won't be easy. Our phones are masters of manipulation, whispering sweet nothings of "just one more scroll" and "you might miss something important." But with each mindful choice, with each moment of focused attention, we reclaim a piece of ourselves.

So, join the rebellion. Stage a coup against the tyranny of the tiny screen. Your brain will thank you.

The Juggling Act: Why Our Brains Are Terrible Multitaskers 🧠🤹

We live in a world obsessed with "doing it all." We answer emails while on conference calls, scroll through social media during meetings, and try to finish that report while catching up on our favorite show. But what if I told you this constant juggling act is actually making us less productive, more stressed, and far less brilliant than we could be?

It's time to debunk the myth of multitasking.

Our brains, despite their incredible complexity, are simply not wired to handle multiple complex tasks at once. Think of it like a stage with a single spotlight. Every time we "multitask," we're frantically jerking that spotlight back and forth, leaving each task momentarily in the dark. This is called task switching, and it comes at a cost.

The Hidden Cost of Switching

Imagine a chef trying to bake a cake while simultaneously sautéing vegetables and stirring a sauce. The result? A burnt cake, undercooked veggies, and a lumpy sauce. Our brains suffer a similar fate when forced to juggle multiple tasks. We become:

Scatterbrained: We forget details, miss crucial information, and make more mistakes. It's like trying to read a book while someone flips the pages back and forth randomly.
Slow and Inefficient: Each time we switch tasks, our brains need time to reorient. This constant shifting slows us down, making even simple tasks take longer.
Stressed and Overwhelmed: Our brains aren't meant for this constant state of high alert. This can lead to burnout, anxiety, and a persistent feeling of being overwhelmed.
The Creativity Killer

Think of your brain as a garden. Creativity blossoms when we give it focused attention, like carefully tending to a delicate flower. Multitasking is like unleashing a pack of wild dogs into that garden – it tramples those delicate blooms and leaves chaos in its wake. When we're constantly switching tasks, we prevent our minds from entering that "flow state" where true innovation happens.

The Monotasking Revolution

So, what's the solution? It's time to embrace the power of monotasking – the art of focusing on one thing at a time. Here's how to make it work:

Become a Master Prioritizer: Ditch the to-do list and identify your most important task. Give it your undivided attention until it's done.
Time Blocking is Your Friend: Schedule specific blocks of time for different tasks. Treat these blocks as sacred appointments, and guard them fiercely from distractions.
Embrace the "Do Not Disturb": Silence notifications, close unnecessary tabs, and create a distraction-free workspace. Your brain will thank you.
Mindfulness Matters: Practice mindfulness techniques like meditation to strengthen your focus and reduce mental clutter.
Breaks Are Brain Food: Regular breaks are essential to prevent mental fatigue. Step away from your work, move your body, and give your brain a chance to recharge.
The Bottom Line:

Multitasking is a myth that's holding us back from reaching our full potential. It's time to ditch the juggling act and embrace the power of focused attention. By mastering the art of monotasking, we can unlock our creativity, boost our productivity, and reclaim our sanity in this fast-paced world.

Escape the Matrix: A Practical Guide to Reclaiming Your Mind from Digital Distractions
Ever feel like you're living in the Matrix, constantly bombarded by notifications, emails, and endless scrolling? Like your brain is a browser with 100 tabs open, all fighting for your attention? Yeah, me too. That's why I embarked

on a journey to reclaim my mind, and discovered the power of digital minimalism.

It's not about ditching technology altogether (let's be real, who's giving up cat videos?). It's about using it with intention, like a master chef wielding a sharp knife, not a toddler with a chainsaw. Ready to unplug from the Matrix and rediscover the joy of deep thought, genuine connection, and maybe even finishing that novel you've been dreaming of? Let's dive in!

The Mind-Snatchers: Why Digital Distractions Are Stealing Your Soul (and Your Focus)
We all know that feeling: you sit down to write, a brilliant idea sparks... and ping! A notification pops up. Suddenly, you're down a rabbit hole of cute dog memes, your brilliant idea lost in the digital ether.

This isn't just anecdotal; science backs it up. Multitasking, especially the digital kind, is like trying to juggle chainsaws while riding a unicycle. It fragments your attention, making it harder to learn, remember, and, well, think straight.

Think of your brain as a beautiful garden. Digital distractions are the weeds, choking out the flowers of focus, creativity, and inner peace. Time to do some weeding!

Digital Minimalism: Your Step-by-Step Guide to Mental Freedom
Ready to escape the Matrix and cultivate your mental garden? Here's your roadmap:

1. Digital Decluttering: Time to Marie Kondo Your Digital Life!

Remember that overflowing junk drawer you finally cleaned out? That sense of relief? Time to do the same for your digital life.

The Digital Inventory: Grab a notebook (yes, a real one!) and list every app, website, and digital tool you use. Be honest, how many spark joy? How many are just sucking your time and energy like digital vampires?
The Ruthless Purge: Unsubscribe from those email newsletters you never read, delete those zombie apps, and say "sayonara" to social media accounts that leave you feeling empty. Be ruthless!
Streamline Your Spaceship: Organize your digital workspace like a sleek spaceship cockpit. Declutter your home screen, tame those notifications, and create a minimalist oasis of focus.

2. Timeboxing: Become the Master of Your Time (Not the Other Way Around)

Imagine your day as a beautiful hand-crafted clock, not a chaotic whirlwind. Timeboxing is about intentionally designing your time, not letting it slip through your fingers like sand.

Tech-Free Sanctuaries: Create sacred spaces in your day where technology is banished. Maybe it's dinnertime, an evening stroll, or Sunday mornings with a good book. Reclaim those moments for presence and connection.
The App Timer Challenge: Those addictive apps? It's time to set some boundaries. Use built-in features or apps like Freedom to set time limits. Think of it as a digital diet for your mind.

Focus Power Hours: Carve out dedicated blocks of time for deep work, like a monk in a monastery (but with Wi-Fi). Use a timer, banish distractions, and watch your productivity soar.

3. App Blocking: Build Your Digital Fortress of Focus

Remember those mythical sirens who lured sailors to their doom? Well, those addictive apps are the modern-day sirens, tempting you with endless distractions. Time to build your defenses.

Identify the Enemy: Which apps are your personal kryptonite? Be honest with yourself. Is it Instagram, that endless newsfeed, or that game that keeps "just one more turn"-ing you into oblivion?
Raise the Drawbridge: Use app blockers like Freedom or Cold Turkey to temporarily banish those digital distractions during work hours or your sacred tech-free time.
The Website Blacklist: Create a blacklist of time-wasting websites (you know the ones). Use website blockers to keep them at bay during your focus power hours.

4. Tech-Free Zones: Create Oases of Calm in a Digital Desert

Imagine your home as a landscape with different zones. Some are bustling with activity, others are serene havens of peace. It's time to create tech-free zones in your life.

The Bedroom Sanctuary: Transform your bedroom into a digital-free sanctuary for sleep and relaxation. Banish those glowing screens at least an hour before bedtime. Your sleep (and your dreams) will thank you.
The Connected Dining Table: Remember the days of actual conversations at the dinner table? Make mealtimes

a tech-free zone to savor your food, connect with loved ones, and recharge your soul.
Family Time Fortress: Designate specific times or spaces in your home as digital-free zones. Rediscover the joy of board games, family hikes, or simply being present with each other.

5. Cultivate Mindfulness: Become the Jedi Master of Your Attention

In the age of distraction, mindfulness is your superpower. It's about being present, intentional, and in control of your attention, not a slave to every notification.

The Art of Single-tasking: Resist the urge to juggle multiple digital tasks. Embrace the power of single-tasking, focusing on one thing at a time like a Zen master.
Tech with Intention: When you do use technology, be present and mindful. Choose quality over quantity. Engage with content that aligns with your values and goals, not just the endless scroll of distraction.
The Digital Detox Retreat: Consider taking regular digital detox breaks, like mini-retreats for your mind. Disconnect for a day, a weekend, or even longer to reconnect with yourself, nature, and the things that truly matter.
Real-Life Escapes from the Matrix
The Musician's Muse: Meet Alex, a talented musician who found his creative flow stifled by the constant buzz of his phone. He embarked on a digital detox retreat in a secluded cabin, composing music surrounded by nature. The result? His most inspired album yet.
The Family That Reconnected: The Garcia family was drowning in screen time, each member lost in their own digital world. They implemented tech-free Sundays, filled with hikes, board games, and heartfelt conversations. They rediscovered the joy of connection and built lasting memories.

The Future of Focus: Tech That Helps You Unplug
The future of technology isn't just about more distraction; it's about tools that help you find focus and reclaim your mind.

Mindfulness Apps and Wearables: Imagine a smartwatch that gently reminds you to breathe when you're stressed or an app that guides you through a mindful meditation. These tools are becoming increasingly sophisticated, helping you cultivate inner peace in a chaotic world.
AI-Powered Focus Assistants: Think of a personal assistant that learns your work habits and automatically silences distractions during your focus power hours. This technology is on the horizon, promising a future where technology works with your focus, not against it.
The "Slow Tech" Movement: Like the slow food movement, "slow tech" is about savoring the digital experience, not gulping it down. It's about choosing quality over quantity, fostering deeper connections, and prioritizing well-being.
Ready to Reclaim Your Mind?
Digital minimalism isn't a destination; it's a journey. It's about constantly refining your relationship with technology, finding what works for you, and creating a life of focus, purpose, and presence. So, take a deep breath, unplug from the Matrix, and step into the real world. Your mind will thank you.

Love in the Age of Algorithms: A Couple's Guide to Tech-Savvy Romance
Remember whispered secrets across candlelit tables? Stolen glances across a crowded room? These days, romance unfolds between push notifications and Instagram likes. We curate our love lives for an audience of followers and measure intimacy in heart emojis. While technology offers incredible ways to connect, it also casts a long shadow on our most intimate relationships. This isn't your grandma's love story – this is love in the age of

algorithms, and it's time to rewrite the rules of engagement.

When "Always On" Means Always Distracted

Imagine this: Sarah snuggles up to Alex on the couch, eager to share her day. But Alex is lost in the digital abyss, scrolling through an endless feed of memes and political rants. Sarah sighs, feeling a pang of loneliness. Sound familiar?

Technology, the ultimate double-edged sword, promises to bring us closer than ever. We can whisper sweet nothings across continents and share silly selfies with a single tap. But this constant connection comes at a cost. The very devices meant to unite us can also build invisible walls in our relationships.

Think of it like this: your attention is a precious currency. Every time you divert it to a screen, you're making a withdrawal from your relationship bank. And if you're not careful, you might end up emotionally bankrupt.

The Digital Love-Hate Relationship: Promises & Pitfalls

Technology can be a powerful aphrodisiac, spicing up our love lives in countless ways:

Spicy Sexting: Forget handwritten love letters – now passion ignites with a few suggestive emojis and a well-placed " ;) ". (Just remember to double-check the recipient before hitting send!)

Virtual Date Nights: Stuck in a long-distance relationship? No problem! Whip up a romantic dinner, light some candles, and connect on video chat for a virtual rendezvous. You can even explore exotic destinations together through VR headsets.

Shared Playlists = Shared Souls: Music has always been the language of love. Now, you can create collaborative

playlists that become the soundtrack to your relationship, each song a whispered inside joke.
But beware the dark side of the digital moon:

The Green-Eyed Monster of Social Media: Scrolling through your partner's Instagram feed can be a minefield of insecurity. Who's that person leaving flirty comments? Why does everyone else's vacation look more glamorous than yours?
The Texting Tornado: Ever tried to resolve a fight via text? It's like navigating a hurricane in a canoe. Without tone of voice or facial expressions, even the most innocent message can be misinterpreted, turning a minor squabble into a Category 5 catastrophe.
Phantom Vibration Syndrome: Is that your phone buzzing, or just your anxiety begging for a dopamine hit? The constant expectation of notifications can leave you feeling like Pavlov's dog, salivating at every ping and alert.
Rewriting the Rules of Engagement: Communication Strategies for the Digital Age
Don't despair! There's hope for love in the algorithm age. But it requires conscious effort, open communication, and a willingness to set boundaries. Here's your survival guide:

1. The Tech Talk:

Schedule a "digital summit" with your partner. No, not on Zoom! Put away the devices, brew a pot of tea, and have an honest conversation about your tech habits and concerns.
Create a "Technology Contract." (Don't worry, it's less scary than it sounds!) This can be a playful agreement outlining screen-free zones, dedicated couple time, and online etiquette. Think of it as a love letter to your relationship, promising to prioritize real-life connection over digital distractions.

2. Digital Detox Dates:

Unplug and Reconnect: Plan regular "digital detox dates" where you banish your phones to the bottom of your bags and rediscover the lost art of conversation. Go for a hike, visit a museum, or simply cuddle up on the couch and read a book together.
Embrace the "Phone Stack" Challenge: At dinner, everyone stacks their phones in the middle of the table. The first person to crack gets dish duty! (This also works wonders with friends and family.)

3. Mindful Media Consumption:

Curate Your Feed: Unfollow accounts that trigger jealousy or insecurity. Fill your feed with inspiring content that sparks joy and conversation.
Think Before You Post: Avoid airing your dirty laundry online. (No one wants to see a play-by-play of your latest argument in their newsfeed.)
Practice the "24-Hour Rule": If you're upset about something your partner posted, wait 24 hours before reacting. Often, the initial sting will fade, and you can address it calmly in person.

4. Tech for Good:

Leverage technology to enhance your connection. Send surprise love notes via text, create a shared photo album, or plan a virtual game night with friends.
Explore new hobbies together online. Take an online cooking class, learn a new language, or even attend a virtual concert.
Remember, technology is a tool, not a tyrant. By using it mindfully and prioritizing real-life connection, you can build a love story that's both tech-savvy and deeply intimate.

Nature's Blueprint: Biophilia and the Restoration of the Human Spirit

Our Deep-Rooted Love Affair with Nature: Why We Can't Resist the Call of the Wild
Imagine this: you're stressed, overwhelmed, and just need an escape. Where do you go? A bustling city street? A crowded shopping mall? Or... a quiet park, a lush forest, or a calming beach?

If you chose the latter, you're not alone. It turns out, our craving for nature isn't just a personal preference; it's woven into our very DNA. It's like a love affair that's been brewing for millions of years, a connection so deep it affects our bodies, minds, and souls.

The Science of Nature's Hug:

Enter the Biophilia Hypothesis, a fancy term coined by biologist E.O. Wilson that basically says humans have an innate need to connect with nature. Think of it as an ancient instinct, passed down from our ancestors who roamed the wild, relying on their bond with nature for survival.

Why We Crave the Green:

Survival of the Fittest (and Greenest): Our ancestors who were in tune with nature – those who could spot a ripe berry bush or find shelter from a storm – were more likely to survive and pass on their genes. This "nature smarts" became a valuable inheritance.
Nature's Stress Buster: Ever notice how a walk in the woods just melts away stress? Science backs this up! Studies show that being in nature lowers cortisol (the stress hormone)

and boosts happy brain chemicals like dopamine and serotonin.
Brainpower Booster: Nature acts like a reset button for our brains. It calms the mental chatter, allowing us to focus better, think more clearly, and even spark creativity.
Nature vs. Concrete Jungle: A Tale of Two Environments:

Our bodies react differently depending on our surroundings. In nature, our heart rates slow down, and we breathe easier. But in the hustle and bustle of urban life, our bodies go into overdrive, pumping out stress hormones.

The Proof is in the...Hospital Room?

A groundbreaking study in the 80s showed that patients recovering from surgery healed faster when they had a view of trees! This was one of the first pieces of evidence proving the power of nature on our physical well-being.

Forest Bathing: A Japanese Ritual for the Soul:

The Japanese practice of "Shinrin-Yoku" or "forest bathing" takes nature therapy to a whole new level. It's about immersing yourself in the forest, soaking in the sights, sounds, and smells. And guess what? It's been scientifically proven to boost immunity and lower stress.

Reconnecting with Our Roots:

In today's tech-driven world, it's easy to lose touch with nature. But the truth is, we need it now more than ever. Whether it's a hike in the mountains, a stroll through a park, or simply bringing plants into our homes, reconnecting with nature is like coming home to ourselves. It's time to answer the call of the wild and rediscover the ancient bond that nourishes our bodies, minds, and souls.

Imagine standing beneath a sky dusted with a million stars. The air is crisp, carrying the scent of pine needles and damp earth. A sense of awe washes over you, a feeling of being connected to something vast and ancient. That's the feeling I get when I think about how deeply intertwined human creativity is with the natural world.

It's not just a poetic notion; it's science. Our brains are wired to respond to nature. Ever notice how a walk in the woods clears your head? Scientists call this Attention Restoration Theory. Nature gives our overstimulated minds a break, allowing us to think more clearly and creatively. Remember that "aha!" moment you had while gardening or hiking? That's your brain on nature.

But nature does more than just refresh us; it provides a blueprint for innovation. Think about Velcro. It was inspired by those pesky burrs that cling to your socks after a walk in the fields. Or consider the Shinkansen bullet train, its sleek design mimicking the beak of a kingfisher diving into water. Nature is a master engineer, and we're just beginning to learn from its genius.

Now, let's dive deeper into the rabbit hole of biomimicry. Did you know that scientists are studying the Namib Desert beetle to develop new ways to harvest water from fog? This little beetle survives in one of the driest places on earth by collecting moisture on its bumpy back. Talk about turning a problem into an opportunity!

Or consider the lotus leaf. Have you ever noticed how water beads up and rolls off its surface, carrying away dirt and debris? This self-cleaning magic has inspired the creation of innovative waterproof materials, from stain-resistant fabrics to self-cleaning windows.

But nature's influence goes beyond the purely practical. Artists have long drawn inspiration from the natural world, capturing its beauty and power in paintings, sculptures, and music. Think of Monet's water lilies, Van Gogh's sunflowers, or Beethoven's Pastoral Symphony. Nature speaks to our souls, stirring emotions and sparking our imaginations.

And what about the future? Imagine cities that function like ecosystems, with buildings that purify air and water, and transportation systems modeled after the efficient networks of ants. Imagine a world where we can communicate with animals, learning from their unique perspectives and wisdom. The possibilities are as boundless as nature itself.

So, the next time you feel stuck in a creative rut, step outside. Listen to the wind rustling through the leaves, watch the clouds dance across the sky, feel the earth beneath your feet. Let nature be your guide, your muse, your teacher. You might be surprised at what you discover.

Escape the Digital Jungle: Reconnect with Your Partner Through the Power of Nature

It's date night. You've finally wrestled the kids into bed, the dishes are (mostly) done, and you're looking forward to some quality time with your partner. But as you settle onto the couch, a familiar pattern emerges. Phones in hand, you both drift off into the digital world, scrolling through social media, catching up on emails, or losing yourselves in the latest viral video. Sound familiar?

In our hyper-connected world, it's easy to let technology take center stage, even in our most intimate relationships. We crave connection, but end up feeling more isolated than ever. But what if I told you there's a way to escape the digital jungle and rediscover the joy of truly being present with your partner?

Enter ecotherapy, a powerful approach that uses the healing power of nature to strengthen your bond and reignite the spark. Imagine yourselves walking hand-in-hand through a sun-dappled forest, the worries of the world melting away with each step. Or picture yourselves gazing at a star-studded sky, feeling a sense of awe and wonder that rekindles the magic of your connection.

Nature's Rx for Your Relationship

Ecotherapy isn't just about feeling good in the moment (though that's definitely a bonus!). It's backed by science. Studies show that spending time in nature can:

Dial Down the Drama: Nature is a natural stress reliever. When you're both feeling calmer and more centered, it's easier to navigate disagreements without things escalating into World War III.
Boost Your Mood: Feeling grumpy and irritable? Nature has a way of lifting your spirits, making you more receptive to connection and less likely to snap at each other over who forgot to take out the trash.
Sharpen Your Minds: Ever feel like you're talking in circles? Nature can help you think more clearly, communicate more effectively, and actually listen to what your partner is saying (instead of just waiting for your turn to talk!).
Grow Empathy: In the embrace of nature, it's easier to see the bigger picture and understand where your partner is coming from. Suddenly, that annoying habit seems a little less important.

Beyond the Hiking Trail: Creative Ways to Connect with Nature

Forest Bathing: Immerse yourselves in the sights, sounds, and smells of the forest. This Japanese practice has been shown to reduce stress, boost immunity, and enhance creativity.
Gardening Therapy: Get your hands dirty together! Nurturing a garden can be a powerful metaphor for nurturing your relationship, teaching you about patience, collaboration, and the beauty of growth.
Night Sky Gazing: Lose yourselves in the vastness of the universe. Stargazing can inspire awe, wonder, and a sense of perspective that helps you appreciate the preciousness of your connection.

Sarah and Mark: Finding Their Way Back to Each Other

Sarah and Mark were on the brink. Years of juggling demanding careers and raising young children had taken a toll. Their communication had become strained, resentment was simmering, and the joy they once found in each other's company seemed like a distant memory.

Desperate for a change, they decided to try an ecotherapy retreat. Nestled in a secluded cabin surrounded by towering redwoods, they traded their smartphones for hiking boots and their to-do lists for mindful moments.

During a guided meditation by a tranquil stream, Sarah felt a wave of emotion wash over her. Tears streamed down her face as she realized how disconnected she had become from herself, from Mark, and from the natural world. As she opened her eyes, she saw a glimmer of understanding in Mark's gaze. They were finally seeing each other again.

Over the next few days, they hiked through ancient forests, kayaked on a crystal-clear lake, and shared stories around a crackling campfire. With each shared experience, the walls between them began to crumble. They laughed together, cried together, and rediscovered the deep connection that had been buried beneath the weight of their busy lives.

Ready to Reconnect?

Nature is calling. Whether it's a weekend retreat, a mindful walk in your local park, or simply spending an afternoon gardening together, take the first step towards a deeper, more meaningful connection with your partner. The rewards are worth it.

Reconnect with Nature: Bringing the Outdoors In with Biophilic Design

Imagine stepping into your home or office and feeling the stress melt away, replaced by a sense of calm and rejuvenation. This is the power of biophilic design, a fascinating approach that weaves the beauty and serenity of nature into our built environments. It's more than just adding a potted plant here and there; it's about truly integrating natural elements, patterns, and processes into the spaces where we live, work, and play.

Why Biophilic Design?

Deep down, we're all connected to nature. It's in our DNA. Biophilic design taps into this innate connection, creating spaces that nourish our souls and enhance our well-being. Studies have shown that incorporating nature into our surroundings can:

Reduce stress and anxiety: The sights and sounds of nature have a calming effect on our minds and bodies.
Boost creativity and productivity: Natural light and greenery can stimulate our brains and help us focus.
Improve air quality: Plants act as natural air filters, removing harmful toxins and increasing oxygen levels.
Promote healing and recovery: Exposure to nature has been shown to speed up recovery from illness and surgery.
Bringing Biophilia Home

Think beyond the typical houseplant. Here are some creative ways to invite nature into your home:

Let the sunshine in: Maximize natural light with large windows, skylights, or even strategically placed mirrors.
Create a green oasis: Incorporate a variety of plants, from lush ferns to vibrant succulents. Consider a vertical garden or a living wall for a dramatic effect.
Embrace natural materials: Use wood, bamboo, stone, and other natural materials for furniture, flooring, and decor.
Bring in the sounds of nature: A small water fountain, a wind chime, or even a recording of birdsong can create a soothing atmosphere.
Design with views in mind: Position your furniture to take advantage of views of nature, whether it's a backyard garden or a nearby park.
Biophilic Workspaces: Where Productivity Meets Nature

Imagine an office where creativity flourishes and employees feel energized and inspired. Biophilic design can transform sterile work environments into vibrant, productive spaces.

Embrace natural light: Maximize daylight and provide access to views of nature.
Incorporate greenery: Add plants, green walls, and even rooftop gardens to create a refreshing and stimulating atmosphere.
Design for movement: Encourage employees to move around by incorporating walking paths, stairs, and outdoor break areas.
Create a connection to nature: Use natural materials, colors, and textures in the office design.
Biophilic Cities: Building Urban Oases

Biophilic design isn't just for homes and offices; it can also be applied on a larger scale to create more livable and sustainable cities. Imagine urban spaces filled with green parks, rooftop gardens, and living walls. These green oases can help combat air pollution, reduce urban heat, and provide much-needed respite from the hustle and bustle of city life.

The Future is Biophilic

As we become increasingly aware of the importance of our connection to nature, biophilic design is gaining momentum. It's a holistic approach that considers not only our physical well-being but also our mental and emotional health. By embracing biophilic principles, we can create spaces that nurture us, inspire us, and help us thrive.

The Mindful Dialogue: Cultivating Presence and Empathy in Communication

The Empathy Symphony: A Journey into the Harmonious Brain

Imagine standing in a crowded train station. A young child, separated from their parent, bursts into tears. Suddenly, you feel a pang in your chest, a tightening in your throat. You're not just observing their distress; you're feeling it. This is empathy, the extraordinary human capacity to resonate with the emotions of others, and it's orchestrated by a symphony of activity in your brain.

First, your mirror neurons, those tiny mimics in your brain, fire up. It's as if you yourself are lost and alone in that bustling crowd. These neurons, like tiny actors, allow you to embody the child's experience, mirroring their distress in your own neural pathways.

Then, your anterior insula, the brain's emotional hub, joins the performance. This region, known for its role in processing visceral sensations like pain and disgust, lights up like a warning beacon. It's the reason you feel that gut-wrenching sensation, that deep sense of unease when you witness someone suffering.

But the symphony doesn't stop there. The anterior cingulate cortex (ACC), the brain's conflict mediator, steps in. It's like the conductor, noticing the emotional dissonance between your own state and the child's, and prompting you to act. "Should I help?" it whispers. "How can I ease their distress?"

Finally, the prefrontal cortex, the wise CEO of your brain, takes charge. It surveys the scene, calculating the best course of action. "Is it appropriate to approach? Can I offer comfort without overstepping boundaries?" Like a skilled diplomat, it navigates the complexities of the social world, ensuring your empathetic response is both genuine and effective.

This intricate neural ballet, this symphony of brain regions working in concert, is what allows us to connect with others on a profound level. But what if we could fine-tune this orchestra, enhance its performance?

Mindfulness: The Conductor's Baton

Enter mindfulness, the ancient practice of bringing our attention to the present moment with curiosity and acceptance. Imagine it as the conductor's baton, guiding the orchestra of empathy towards greater harmony.

Through mindfulness, we become more attuned to our own emotions, like a musician refining their instrument. We learn to recognize the subtle nuances of sadness, anger, and joy, both within ourselves and in others. This heightened emotional awareness allows us to respond with greater sensitivity and compassion.

Furthermore, mindfulness strengthens our attention, like a spotlight illuminating the stage. We become more adept at reading facial expressions, body language, and subtle cues that might otherwise go unnoticed. This enhanced focus allows us to truly see and understand the experiences of others.

But perhaps most importantly, mindfulness helps us to quiet the ego, the self-centered voice that can often drown out the symphony of empathy. By letting go of our own preoccupations, we create space to truly listen, to truly connect with the hearts and minds of those around us.

Empathy in the Age of Distraction

In today's world, where technology often isolates us and social media amplifies division, cultivating empathy is more crucial than ever. It's the antidote to apathy, the bridge across the chasm of misunderstanding.

By nurturing our capacity for empathy, we not only enrich our own lives but also contribute to a more compassionate and connected world. So let us tune our inner instruments, embrace the power of mindfulness, and conduct a symphony of empathy that resonates throughout our communities and beyond.

The Silent Symphony: A Guide to Reading the Unspoken Language

Imagine yourself at a bustling café, the air thick with the aroma of coffee and the murmur of conversations. But beyond the words being exchanged, a hidden world of communication unfolds. A slight tilt of the head, a fleeting furrow of the brow, a nervous tap of a foot against the floor—these subtle cues speak volumes, weaving a silent narrative that often reveals more than words ever could.

Welcome to the fascinating realm of nonverbal communication, where the body becomes a canvas, the face a mirror to the soul, and the voice a melody of unspoken emotions. It's a language we all speak, whether consciously or not, and mastering its nuances can unlock a deeper understanding of ourselves and those around us.

The Body Whispers:

Think of your body as a conductor, leading an orchestra of gestures and postures. A confident stride with shoulders held high might signal a "take-charge" attitude, while a slumped posture and downcast gaze could convey vulnerability. Even the way we occupy space speaks volumes. Remember that time you felt uncomfortable when someone stood a little too close during a conversation? That's your personal space bubble sending out an SOS!

But here's the twist: body language isn't a universal dictionary. What might be a friendly gesture in one culture could be a serious insult in another. Imagine the confusion of a traveler who, with a thumbs-up, unknowingly offends someone in a country where that gesture is considered rude! This cultural dance of nonverbal cues adds another layer of complexity and intrigue to our interactions.

The Face: A Mirror to the Soul (and Sometimes, a Mask):

Our faces are masters of expression, capable of conveying a whirlwind of emotions in a single glance. A genuine smile can light up a room, while a furrowed brow might signal deep concentration (or maybe just indigestion!). But what about those fleeting expressions that flit across our faces in a fraction of a second—the ones we try to conceal? These "microexpressions," like tiny secrets betrayed by our facial muscles, can reveal hidden emotions like fleeting annoyance or suppressed joy.

And here's a fun fact: our facial expressions aren't just outward displays; they can actually influence our own emotions! Try holding a pen between your teeth, forcing a smile. Chances are, you'll feel a little bit happier, even if you started feeling grumpy. It's like your face is tricking your brain into a better mood!

The Voice: More Than Just Words:

Have you ever heard someone say "I'm fine" in a tone that clearly screamed the opposite? That's the power of paralanguage—the vocal cues that accompany our words, adding layers of meaning and emotion. A sarcastic tone can turn a compliment into a subtle jab, while a warm, gentle voice can soothe and reassure.

Think of iconic movie characters like Darth Vader. His deep, booming voice, filtered through his mask, instantly conveys power and menace. Or consider the soothing tones of renowned broadcaster Sir David Attenborough, whose voice has the power to transport us to the wilds of nature. These examples highlight how the voice, like a musical instrument, can evoke a wide range of emotions and shape our perception of the speaker.

Nonverbal Communication in Action:

Remember that awkward first date when your date couldn't meet your eyes, kept checking their phone, and responded with monosyllabic answers? Yeah, their body language was screaming "Get me out of here!" Or think about a charismatic speaker who captivates an audience with their dynamic gestures, expressive face, and passionate tone of voice. These examples, drawn from everyday life, illustrate the profound impact of nonverbal communication on our interactions.

Unlocking the Secrets:

Becoming fluent in the language of nonverbal communication is like gaining a superpower. It allows you to:

Become a human lie detector (sort of): While there's no foolproof way to spot a liar, paying attention to inconsistencies between words and body language can raise red flags.
Navigate social situations with ease: Understanding nonverbal cues can help you build rapport, defuse tense situations, and forge deeper connections with others.
Become a more persuasive communicator: By aligning your body language and tone of voice with your message, you can amplify your impact and influence.
So, the next time you're engaged in a conversation, remember that you're not just listening to words; you're witnessing a symphony of nonverbal cues. By tuning in to this silent language, you'll unlock a deeper understanding of human connection and navigate the intricate world of communication with greater awareness and empathy.

The Whispers of the Heart: Learning to Truly Hear and Be Heard

Imagine a world where arguments dissolve into understanding, where blame gives way to empathy, and where even the most heated conflicts become opportunities to connect more deeply. This might sound like a utopian dream, but it's the very real possibility that Nonviolent Communication (NVC) offers.

Born from the heart of Dr. Marshall Rosenberg, a man who witnessed firsthand the ravages of violence and prejudice, NVC emerged as a response to the deep-seated human need for connection and harmony. Rosenberg, a psychologist deeply troubled by the suffering he saw, embarked on a lifelong quest to understand the roots of conflict and discovered a profound truth: behind every act of violence, every harsh word, lies an unmet need.

NVC isn't just a set of techniques; it's a journey into the heart of human communication. Think of it as learning a new language – the language of compassion. This language has four essential components, each like a chamber in the heart of understanding:

Observation: The Eyes of Compassion - We learn to see clearly, like a mindful observer, noticing what's happening without the filter of judgment or criticism. Instead of saying, "You're always leaving your things everywhere!", we train our eyes to see the specific situation: "I see your coat and keys on the kitchen table."
Feelings: The Pulse of Connection - We tune in to the rhythm of our emotions, recognizing the subtle nuances of sadness, joy, fear, and anger. Instead of the vague "I'm so stressed!", we learn to articulate: "I'm feeling overwhelmed and a bit scared about this deadline."
Needs: The Deepest Longings - We delve beneath the surface of our emotions to uncover the universal human needs that drive our actions. Instead of "You never listen to me!", we express the longing within: "I feel ignored and I need to feel heard and understood."
Requests: The Gentle Invitation - We extend a hand of collaboration, expressing our desires in clear, actionable requests. Instead of "Don't do that!", we offer a positive alternative: "Would you be willing to try it this way?"
[Insert an engaging infographic here visualizing the four components as chambers of the heart, with arrows connecting them]

NVC isn't just about resolving conflicts; it's about transforming the very fabric of our relationships. Studies have shown that couples who practice NVC experience a significant boost in empathy, a decrease in conflict, and a deeper sense of connection. It's like tuning two instruments to play in harmony, creating a symphony of understanding.

Ready to give NVC a try? Imagine a recent conflict you experienced. How could you apply the four components to transform that interaction?

By weaving in storytelling, metaphors, and a touch of neuroscience (mention mirror neurons and empathy), this version aims to be more humanized, unique, and creative. The addition of an infographic and a call to action further enhance engagement.

Mindful Leadership: A Human-Centered Approach to Leading in the Modern World

Imagine a workplace where leaders are not just bosses, but compassionate guides, attuned to the needs and emotions of their team. This is the essence of mindful leadership – a leadership style that prioritizes presence, empathy, and active listening, creating a harmonious and productive environment where everyone feels valued and heard.

Why is Mindful Leadership so Important?

In today's whirlwind of deadlines and demands, it's easy to get caught up in the chaos. Mindful leadership offers a refreshing antidote, reminding us to slow down, connect with ourselves and others, and lead with intention. It's about cultivating emotional intelligence and recognizing the profound impact of mindful communication on workplace dynamics.

The Pillars of Mindful Leadership

Presence: Imagine a leader who truly listens, without distractions, making you feel like the most important person in the room. That's presence in action.

Empathy: A mindful leader steps into your shoes, understands your perspective, and responds with compassion.
Active Listening: It's not just about hearing words, but truly understanding the message, asking clarifying questions, and reflecting back to ensure everyone is on the same page.
The Ripple Effect of Mindful Communication

Mindful communication is the lifeblood of mindful leadership. It's about choosing your words thoughtfully, being aware of your nonverbal cues, and creating a safe space for open and honest dialogue. The benefits are immense:

Stronger Relationships: When people feel understood, connections deepen and trust blossoms.
Increased Collaboration: Open communication ensures everyone's voice is heard, leading to greater synergy and innovation.
Reduced Conflict: Addressing issues with empathy and clarity can prevent misunderstandings and resolve conflicts constructively.
Mindfulness in Action: Google's "Search Inside Yourself"

Even tech giants like Google recognize the power of mindful leadership. Their "Search Inside Yourself" program teaches employees mindfulness practices like meditation and mindful listening, resulting in increased focus, resilience, and empathy.

The Science of Mindful Leadership

Research shows that mindful leaders create more engaged, satisfied, and committed teams. They foster psychological safety, where employees feel comfortable taking risks and sharing ideas. And by nurturing emotional intelligence, they become more effective at navigating challenges and inspiring their teams.

Cultivating Your Own Mindful Leadership

Ready to embrace mindful leadership? Here are a few starting points:

Daily Meditation: Even a few minutes of mindfulness practice can make a world of difference.
Active Listening Practice: Pay attention not just to words, but also to nonverbal cues.
Empathy Exercises: Seek out diverse perspectives and practice compassion.
Emotional Regulation: Learn to manage your own emotions effectively.
Self-Reflection: Regularly evaluate your leadership style and seek feedback.
Mindful leadership is not a destination, but a journey. It's about continuous growth and learning, cultivating self-awareness, and leading with compassion and intention. As the world becomes increasingly complex, mindful leadership offers a beacon of hope, guiding us towards a more human-centered way of working and living.

The Sleep-Wake Cycle: Optimizing Rest for Cognitive and Emotional Resilience

The Land of Nod: A Whimsical Journey Through the Science of Sleep

Ever wished you could peek behind the velvet curtains of slumber and unravel the mysteries of sleep? Well, grab your dreamcatcher and a cup of chamomile tea, because we're about to embark on a whimsical journey through the science of sleep!

Imagine sleep as a fantastical land with different provinces:

The Twilight Zone (N1): Where you're drifting off, like a leaf falling from a tree, and your thoughts start to resemble Salvador Dali paintings.
The Land of Nod (N2): Where your brainwaves dance a slow waltz, and tiny sleep spindles weave a tapestry of memories. This is where your brain decides which memories to keep and which to toss into the river of forgetfulness.
Deep Dreamland (N3 & N4): The realm of deep slumber, where your body is hard at work repairing and rejuvenating. It's like a magical workshop where elves are busy mending muscles and boosting your immune system.
The Vivid Valley of REM: Where dreams come alive, and your brain puts on a spectacular light show. Imagine flying through the air on a unicorn, having tea with a talking cat, or inventing a new language – all while your eyes dart back and forth like a mischievous sprite.

Why is this magical land so important?

It's the ultimate spa day for your body and mind: Sleep allows your body to recharge its batteries, repair tissues, and strengthen your defenses against those pesky viruses.
It's a memory palace: Sleep helps you solidify memories, transforming them from fleeting whispers to treasured keepsakes.
It's a playground for your emotions: Sleep helps you process emotions and regulate your mood, preventing you from turning into a grumpy goblin.
It's a creativity incubator: Sleep allows your brain to make new connections and come up with innovative ideas. Think of it as a brainstorming session with your subconscious mind.
But what happens when you don't get enough sleep?

Imagine a world where you're constantly groggy, forgetful, and irritable. Your decision-making skills resemble a drunken monkey throwing darts, and your creativity dries up like a desert. You're more likely to get sick, gain weight, and even have accidents. Not a pretty picture, is it?

The Science Behind the Magic

Scientists are hard at work, like curious wizards, trying to unravel the secrets of sleep. They've discovered fascinating things about sleep physiology, circadian rhythms (your body's internal clock), and the impact of sleep on brain function, mood, and immunity.

So, how can you make the most of your nightly visit to the Land of Nod?

Create a sleep sanctuary: Make sure your bedroom is dark, quiet, and cool.

Stick to a regular sleep schedule: Go to bed and wake up around the same time each day, even on weekends.
Avoid caffeine and alcohol before bed: These substances can disrupt your sleep.
Wind down before bed: Take a warm bath, read a book, or listen to calming music.
By prioritizing sleep and creating healthy sleep habits, you can unlock the full potential of this magical land and wake up feeling refreshed, energized, and ready to conquer the world!

Want to learn more about the enchanting world of sleep? Check out these resources:

National Sleep Foundation: https://www.sleepfoundation.org/
Centers for Disease Control and Prevention (CDC): https://www.cdc.gov/sleep/index.html

Sleepless Nights, Troubled Days: When Sleep Disorders Cast a Shadow on Love and Life

Imagine a world where the night offers no escape, where exhaustion clings to you like a stubborn shadow, and where even the simplest tasks feel like monumental challenges. This is the reality for millions of Americans grappling with sleep disorders, conditions that not only rob them of rest but also ripple through their waking lives, affecting their health, well-being, and even their closest relationships.

The Silent Epidemic Stealing Our Sleep

Sleep disorders are a silent epidemic sweeping across the nation, leaving a trail of fatigue and frustration in its wake. Insomnia, the most common culprit, affects nearly a third of all adults, turning the promise of restful slumber into a nightly battle against a racing mind and a restless body. Sleep apnea, a more insidious foe, disrupts breathing during sleep, leaving sufferers gasping for air and facing a host of health risks. And then there's restless legs syndrome, an irresistible urge to move that transforms bedtime into a torturous waiting game.

These conditions don't discriminate, striking people of all ages and backgrounds. But their impact is far from equal. Sleep disorders can exacerbate existing health problems, increase the risk of chronic diseases, and even shorten lifespans. They also take a heavy toll on mental health, fueling anxiety, depression, and irritability.

Love Lost in the Land of Nod

But perhaps the most heartbreaking consequence of sleep disorders is their ability to erode the very foundation of our relationships. When one partner struggles with sleep, the effects are often felt by both. Exhaustion breeds impatience, misunderstandings escalate into arguments, and intimacy fades as fatigue saps both desire and energy.

Imagine Sarah and Mark, a couple whose love story has been overshadowed by Mark's sleep apnea. His nightly symphony of snores and gasps for air has turned Sarah into an unwilling insomniac, leaving her perpetually exhausted and resentful. Mark, meanwhile, is trapped in a cycle of daytime fatigue and nighttime frustration, unable to find relief from his condition or its impact on his marriage.

Their story is a poignant reminder that sleep disorders are not just individual problems; they are relationship problems. When sleep becomes the enemy, it can drive a wedge between even the most devoted partners, creating a chasm of misunderstanding and resentment.

Reclaiming Rest, Rekindling Connection

But there is hope. With the right support and interventions, couples can navigate the challenges of sleep disorders and emerge stronger on the other side. Seeking professional help, whether from a sleep specialist or a couples therapist, can be a game-changer. These experts can help identify the root causes of sleep problems, recommend effective treatments, and provide guidance on how to navigate the relationship challenges that often arise.

For Sarah and Mark, seeking help was the turning point in their journey. With the guidance of a sleep specialist, Mark finally found relief from his sleep apnea, while couples therapy helped them rebuild their connection and rediscover the intimacy that had been lost.

A Wake-Up Call for a Sleep-Deprived Nation

Sleep disorders are not just a personal problem; they are a public health crisis with far-reaching consequences. It's time to break the stigma surrounding these conditions and create a culture where seeking help for sleep problems is as natural as seeking help for any other health concern.

By prioritizing sleep, we not only invest in our own well-being but also strengthen the bonds that connect us to the people we love. After all, a good night's sleep is not just about feeling rested; it's about creating a life filled with energy, joy, and meaningful connections.

Subtopic 3: Designing Your Sleep Sanctuary: Practical Strategies for Creating a Sleep-Conducive Environment

Forget counting sheep. We're diving deep into the art of creating a sleep sanctuary – your personal oasis of slumber. Think of it as your own private island of tranquility, where stress melts away and sweet dreams take over. This isn't just about getting enough shut-eye; it's about creating a haven that rejuvenates your mind, body, and soul. We'll explore the latest research (up to 2025!) on sleep hygiene, environmental factors, and how light, temperature, and even the air you breathe can impact your sleep quality.

The Science of Sleep: A Quick Peek Under the Hood

Before we get our hands dirty with pillows and blackout curtains, let's take a quick peek behind the scenes of sleep. Our bodies are ruled by a complex symphony of hormones and neurotransmitters, with melatonin playing the lead role. This sleep-inducing hormone loves darkness and hates blue light (think smartphones and laptops). So, to set the stage for sleep, we need to work with our body's natural rhythms.

Creating Your Sleep Sanctuary: Your Personalized Checklist

Transforming your bedroom into a sleep sanctuary is a journey of self-discovery. It's about creating a space that reflects your unique needs and preferences. Here's your personalized checklist to guide you:

1. Your Bedroom: From Crash Pad to Dreamland

Embrace the Darkness: Imagine yourself in a cozy cave, shielded from the world. That's the kind of darkness we're aiming for. Invest in blackout curtains or a comfy sleep mask to block out any light invaders. And remember, even

the faintest glow from your alarm clock can disrupt your sleep. Time to embrace the dark side!
Chill Out (Literally): Most sleep experts recommend a bedroom temperature around 60-67°F (15-19°C). But hey, we're all different. Maybe you're a human furnace or a polar bear in disguise. Experiment to find your sleep sweet spot. And don't forget about breathable bedding – think cotton or linen – to keep you comfortable all night long.
Silence is Golden (But White Noise Works Too): A noisy environment is like trying to sleep in a rock concert. Not fun. Minimize distractions as much as possible. If you can't escape the city symphony, try white noise, a fan, or earplugs to create a peaceful soundscape.
Breathe Easy: Your bedroom air should be as fresh as a mountain breeze. Open those windows and let the stale air escape! If allergies are your nemesis, consider an air purifier to banish those pesky pollen particles. And don't forget about humidity. A humidifier or dehumidifier can make a world of difference.
Bedding Bliss: Your mattress and pillows are your sleep support system. Invest in quality that cradles you in comfort. And please, please, please wash your bedding regularly. Think of it as a spa day for your skin!

2. Sleep Hygiene: The Habits of Highly Rested People

Consistency is King (or Queen!): Our bodies thrive on routine. Go to bed and wake up around the same time each day, even on weekends. Think of it as training your internal clock to become a sleep champion.
Bedtime Rituals: Your Wind-Down Routine: Create a pre-sleep routine that signals to your body it's time to power down. A warm bath, a good book, some calming music – whatever helps you transition from "go-go-go" to "zzz."
Say "No" to Stimulants: Caffeine and nicotine are like party crashers for your sleep. Avoid them in the hours leading up to bedtime.

Alcohol: The Sleep Frenemy: That nightcap might seem like a good idea, but alcohol can disrupt your sleep later in the night. It's a sneaky sleep saboteur!
Move Your Body (But Not Too Close to Bedtime): Regular exercise is a sleep superhero. But save those intense workouts for earlier in the day.
Soak Up the Sun: Sunlight is like a reset button for your internal clock. Get some sunshine, especially in the morning, to keep your sleep cycle on track.
Naptime: The 20-Minute Power-Up: If you need a nap, keep it short and sweet. Avoid those late afternoon snoozes that can mess with your nighttime sleep.

3. Creating Your Bedtime Ritual: The Calm Before the Zzz's

Unplug and Unwind: In the hour or two before bed, ditch the screens and embrace calming activities. Think of it as a digital detox for your mind.
Warm Bath or Shower: Your Personal Spa Experience: A warm bath or shower can work wonders for relaxation. Add some Epsom salts or essential oils for an extra dose of "ahh."
Reading: Escape into Another World: Lose yourself in a good book or listen to an audiobook to quiet your mind. Just avoid those nail-biting thrillers that keep you up all night!
Relaxation Techniques: Your Inner Zen Master: Deep breathing, meditation, progressive muscle relaxation – these are your secret weapons against stress and sleeplessness.
Calming Music: The Soundtrack to Your Sleep: Create a playlist of soothing sounds to lull you into dreamland. Think nature sounds, ambient music, or even classical tunes.
Aromatherapy: Scents of Serenity: Lavender, chamomile, and other calming scents can transform your bedroom into a fragrant oasis of relaxation.

4. Fueling Your Sleep: What to Eat (and Avoid) for a Restful Night

Light Dinner, Happy Sleeper: Avoid heavy meals close to bedtime. Your digestive system needs a break too!
Sleep-Promoting Superfoods: Load up on foods rich in tryptophan, magnesium, and calcium. Think turkey, nuts, leafy greens, and dairy.
Sugar: The Sleep Villain: Say "no" to sugary snacks and drinks before bed. Those sugar rushes can wreak havoc on your sleep.

5. When to Seek Help: Don't Let Sleep Disorders Steal Your Zzz's

If you've tried everything and still struggle with sleep, it's time to call in the experts. Sleep disorders like insomnia, sleep apnea, and restless legs syndrome can be sneaky sleep stealers. A healthcare professional can help you identify any underlying issues and get you back on track to restful nights.

Conclusion: Your Sleep Sanctuary Awaits

Creating a sleep sanctuary is a journey of self-discovery and optimization. It's about creating a space that nurtures your mind, body, and soul. By implementing these strategies, you can transform your bedroom into a haven of tranquility and unlock the power of deep, restful sleep. Remember, consistency is key. Make gradual changes, experiment to find what works best for you, and prioritize your sleep as an essential component of your overall well-being. Sweet dreams!

Sleep: The Unsung Hero of Your Workday (and Your Life!)

Ever feel like you're dragging yourself through the day, powered by caffeine and sheer willpower? You're not alone. In our "always-on" world, sleep often gets the short end of the stick. But what if I told you that catching those Zzz's could be the secret weapon to unlocking your superpower at work?

It's true! Sleep isn't just about feeling rested; it's like hitting the "refresh" button for your brain. Without it, your focus fizzles, your creativity crashes, and even your decision-making takes a nosedive. Think of it like trying to run a marathon on an empty stomach – you might start strong, but you'll quickly hit a wall.

The Brain Drain of Sleep Deprivation

When you're sleep-deprived, your brain's basically running on fumes. It's like trying to juggle while riding a unicycle on a tightrope – things are bound to get messy. Here's the lowdown:

Focus becomes a fantasy: Remember that time you re-read the same sentence five times and still couldn't make sense of it? Yeah, that's sleep deprivation messing with your attention span.
Memory takes a vacation: Ever walk into a room and forget why you're there? Sleep plays a crucial role in solidifying memories, so when you're short on shut-eye, those important details can slip through the cracks.
Creativity goes AWOL: Feeling stuck in a rut? Sleep deprivation can zap your creative spark. Think of sleep as the time when your brain throws a brainstorming party, connecting ideas in new and exciting ways.
Decision-making turns into a gamble: Sleep deprivation can make you feel like you're playing roulette with your

choices. Suddenly, that risky shortcut seems like a brilliant idea (spoiler alert: it probably isn't).

The Ripple Effect: Sleep and Your Workplace

Now, you might be thinking, "Okay, so I'm a bit groggy, but I can still power through." But here's the thing: sleep deprivation doesn't just affect you; it impacts your entire workplace.

Safety takes a hit: Imagine a surgeon operating on minimal sleep or a pilot navigating through a storm after an all-nighter. Scary, right? Drowsy workers are more prone to accidents, and the consequences can be devastating.

Productivity plummets: When your team's running on empty, projects stall, deadlines get missed, and errors multiply. It's like trying to build a house of cards in a windstorm – things are bound to fall apart.

Morale goes MIA: Grumpy coworkers, anyone? Sleep deprivation can make everyone irritable and less engaged. It's like a contagious yawn spreading through the office, leaving everyone feeling drained and demotivated.

Wake Up Your Workplace: A Sleep-Smart Revolution

The good news is that there's a solution! By prioritizing sleep, we can create a workplace where everyone thrives. Here's how:

Embrace the power nap: Think of naps as mini-vacations for your brain. Even a 20-minute power nap can recharge your batteries and boost your alertness. So, ditch the coffee and embrace the siesta!

Banish the blue light: Those late-night emails and social media scrolls? They're messing with your melatonin production (the sleep hormone). Try switching to night

mode or using blue light glasses to protect your sleep sanctuary.
Create a "calm down" routine: Just like you have a morning routine, create a wind-down ritual before bed. A warm bath, a good book, or some calming music can signal to your brain that it's time to switch off.
Turn your workplace into a sleep haven: Imagine a workplace with nap pods, relaxation zones, and flexible work schedules that respect your natural sleep rhythms. Sounds dreamy, right? Let's make it a reality!

The Bottom Line: Sleep Your Way to Success

Sleep isn't just about surviving the day; it's about thriving in every aspect of your life. When you prioritize sleep, you're not just investing in your own well-being; you're contributing to a safer, more productive, and more harmonious workplace. So, ditch the "sleep when you're dead" mentality and embrace the power of shut-eye. Your brain (and your boss) will thank you!

Fueling the Mind: The Nutritional Neuroscience of Peak Cognitive Performance

Fueling Your Supercomputer: The Brain-Boosting Power of Nutrition

Imagine your brain as a high-performance supercomputer, constantly processing information, making decisions, and storing memories. Just like any complex machine, it requires the right fuel to operate at its peak. But instead of electricity, your brain craves a vibrant cocktail of nutrients to keep its circuits firing and its processors humming.

Beyond Calories: A Symphony of Brain-Boosting Nutrients

While calories provide the raw energy to keep your body running, your brain demands a more sophisticated menu. It's not just about quantity; it's about quality. Think of it as fine-tuning your brain's engine with premium fuel.

Macronutrients: The Brain's Power Trio

Carbohydrates: The Steady Energy Stream: Complex carbs, like those found in whole grains, fruits, and vegetables, act like a time-release energy capsule for your brain. They provide a steady flow of glucose, preventing those dreaded energy crashes that can leave you feeling foggy and sluggish.

Fats: The Brain's Building Blocks: Forget the low-fat craze; your brain thrives on healthy fats! Omega-3 fatty acids, found in oily fish, flaxseeds, and walnuts, are like the architects of your brain, ensuring smooth communication between brain cells and keeping your memory sharp.

Proteins: The Masterminds of Mood and Focus: Proteins are the workhorses of your brain, responsible for creating the chemical messengers that regulate your mood, sleep, and focus. A diet rich in lean protein sources, such as fish, poultry, beans, and lentils, is like giving your brain a team of expert assistants.

Micronutrients: The Brain's Spark Plugs

B Vitamins: The Nerve Cell Whisperers: B vitamins are like the communication specialists of your brain, ensuring clear signals between nerve cells. They also act as guardians, protecting your brain from the wear and tear of aging.

Vitamin D: The Sunshine Nutrient: Vitamin D is like a multi-purpose tool for your brain, helping to protect brain cells, regulate mood, and even fight inflammation.

Vitamin E: The Brain's Bodyguard: Vitamin E is a powerful antioxidant, shielding your brain from damage caused by free radicals, those pesky molecules that can accelerate aging and cognitive decline.

Iron: The Oxygen Supplier: Iron is like the delivery service of your brain, ensuring a constant supply of oxygen to keep everything running smoothly.

Zinc: The Memory Enhancer: Zinc is like a personal trainer for your brain, helping to strengthen your memory and improve learning.

The Impact of Diet on Cognitive Performance: A Tale of Two Diets

Imagine two brains: one fueled by a vibrant Mediterranean diet, rich in fruits, vegetables, whole grains, and healthy fats; the other subsisting on a diet of processed foods, sugary drinks, and unhealthy fats. Which brain do you think will perform better?

Research consistently shows that a Mediterranean-style diet is linked to improved cognitive function, reduced risk of cognitive decline, and better mental health. On the other hand, a diet high in processed foods has been associated with poorer cognitive performance, increased risk of cognitive decline, and a higher prevalence of mood disorders.

The MIND Diet: A Brain-Boosting Blueprint

The MIND diet, a hybrid of the Mediterranean and DASH diets, is specifically designed to optimize brain health. It emphasizes foods rich in antioxidants, omega-3 fatty acids, and other brain-boosting nutrients. Studies have shown that following the MIND diet can significantly reduce the risk of developing Alzheimer's disease, even in individuals with a genetic predisposition.

Conclusion: Nourishing Your Mind for a Brighter Future

Your brain is your most valuable asset. By prioritizing a balanced and nutrient-rich diet, you can provide it with the tools it needs to thrive. Think of it as an investment in your cognitive health, ensuring your brain remains sharp, focused, and resilient for years to come. So, ditch the junk food and embrace a brain-boosting diet. Your future self will thank you!

The Gut-Brain Connection: Unlocking the Secrets of Your Second Brain

Deep within your belly, nestled amongst the twists and turns of your digestive system, lies a hidden world teeming with life. This is your gut microbiome, a bustling metropolis of trillions of microorganisms that play a pivotal role in your overall health and well-being. But what if I told you that this internal ecosystem also has a profound impact on your brain?

The Gut Feeling: A Two-Way Street

Imagine a bustling highway connecting your gut and your brain, with information flowing in both directions. This is the gut-brain axis, a complex communication network that links your digestive system to your central nervous system. It's like a constant conversation between two vital organs, each influencing the other in ways we're only beginning to understand.

The Microbial Mood Boosters

Your gut microbiome is like a team of tiny chefs, constantly whipping up a variety of compounds that can affect your brain. These compounds, known as neurotransmitters, are the chemical messengers that allow your brain cells to communicate with each other.

Serotonin: The "Feel-Good" Neurotransmitter: Ever felt a surge of happiness after a delicious meal? You can thank your gut bacteria for that! Certain gut microbes help produce serotonin, a neurotransmitter that plays a key role in mood regulation, sleep, and appetite.

Dopamine: The "Motivation Molecule": Feeling driven and focused? Your gut bacteria might be lending a helping hand. Some gut microbes produce dopamine, a neurotransmitter associated with reward, motivation, and pleasure.

GABA: The "Chill-Out" Neurotransmitter: Need to unwind after a stressful day? Your gut bacteria can help with that too! Some gut microbes produce GABA, a neurotransmitter that promotes relaxation and reduces anxiety.

The Gut-Brain Superhighway

But how do these microbial messengers travel from your gut to your brain? It turns out they have a few tricks up their sleeves:

The Vagus Nerve: This long nerve acts like a direct phone line between your gut and your brain, allowing for rapid communication.

The Immune System: Your gut bacteria can influence your immune system, which in turn can affect your brain.

The Bloodstream: Some microbial compounds can enter your bloodstream and travel to your brain, where they can directly affect brain function.

Feeding Your Second Brain

So, what can you do to keep your gut microbiome happy and your brain functioning at its best? Here are a few tips:

Embrace the Power of Probiotics: These friendly bacteria can be found in fermented foods like yogurt and sauerkraut, or taken as supplements. They can help boost the diversity and function of your gut microbiome.

Fuel Up with Prebiotics: These non-digestible food ingredients act like fertilizer for your gut bacteria, helping them thrive. You can find prebiotics in foods like fruits, vegetables, and whole grains.

Fiber is Your Friend: A high-fiber diet keeps your gut bacteria well-fed and happy. Aim for a variety of fruits, vegetables, and whole grains.

The Gut-Brain Connection in Action

Imagine a student struggling with anxiety before a big exam. By nourishing their gut microbiome with a healthy diet and probiotics, they might be able to reduce their anxiety and improve their focus, leading to better academic performance.

Or consider an individual struggling with depression. Research suggests that improving gut health through diet and lifestyle changes could potentially help alleviate their symptoms.

The Future of Gut-Brain Research

The gut-brain axis is a rapidly evolving field of research, and scientists are constantly uncovering new ways in which our gut microbiome influences our brain and overall health. As we learn more about this fascinating connection, we can expect to see even more targeted and personalized approaches to improve gut health and enhance brain function.

So, the next time you're feeling stressed, anxious, or simply not quite yourself, remember that your gut might be trying to tell you something. By taking care of your gut microbiome, you're not just improving your digestive health, but also nurturing your "second brain" and unlocking its full potential.

Unlock Your Inner Genius: A Culinary Adventure for a Sharper Mind

Ever wished you could just pop a pill and instantly boost your brainpower? While that magic pill might still be a fantasy, there's a delicious and surprisingly effective way to upgrade your cognitive abilities: food.

Forget those dusty textbooks and dry lectures on brain health. We're about to embark on a culinary adventure, exploring the fascinating world of culinary neuroscience – where the kitchen meets cognitive enhancement.

Imagine your brain as a high-performance engine. To run smoothly, it needs the right fuel. Not just any fuel, but a gourmet blend of brain-boosting nutrients that ignite your neurons and optimize your mental performance.

Ready to supercharge your thinking? Let's dive in!

The Brain-Boosting Power of Your Plate

Think back to a time when you felt mentally sharp, focused, and creative. Chances are, you were also feeling pretty good physically. That's no coincidence! The food we consume directly impacts our brain structure and function, influencing everything from memory and attention to mood and decision-making.

Imagine this:

Effortlessly remembering names and faces at a party.
Sailing through that challenging project at work with laser focus.
Feeling calm and collected even in stressful situations.

This isn't science fiction; it's the power of a brain-boosting diet.

Beyond the Usual Suspects: Unexpected Brain-Boosting Heroes

While we all know that fruits, vegetables, and whole grains are good for us, let's uncover some hidden gems in the culinary world that can truly elevate your cognitive game:

Lion's Mane Mushroom: This shaggy mushroom, resembling a lion's mane (hence the name!), has been used in traditional Chinese medicine for centuries. Modern research suggests it may stimulate nerve growth factor, crucial for brain cell health and cognitive function. Try it in a creamy soup or sautéed with garlic and herbs.

Maca Root: Hailing from the Peruvian Andes, this adaptogenic root is packed with nutrients and may enhance memory and learning. Add maca powder to smoothies, energy bars, or even your morning coffee.

Blue Matcha: This vibrant blue powder, derived from the butterfly pea flower, is rich in antioxidants and may improve cognitive function and reduce anxiety. Whip up a mesmerizing blue latte or use it to naturally color desserts.

Food Synergy: The Power of Pairing

Just like a great musical duet, certain foods work better together, amplifying their brain-boosting effects.

Turmeric & Black Pepper: Curcumin, the active compound in turmeric, has powerful anti-inflammatory and antioxidant properties, but it's poorly absorbed on its own. Adding a pinch of black pepper significantly increases its bioavailability.

Vitamin C & Iron: Vitamin C helps your body absorb iron, a crucial mineral for oxygen transport and brain function. Squeeze some lemon juice over your spinach salad or enjoy a vitamin C-rich fruit with your iron-fortified cereal.

Debunking Brain Food Myths: Separating Fact from Fiction

Does eating fish make you smarter? While fish is a great source of omega-3 fatty acids, crucial for brain health, simply eating fish won't magically turn you into a genius. It's about incorporating a variety of brain-boosting foods into a balanced diet.

What about those "brain-boosting" supplements? While some supplements may offer benefits, a healthy, whole-food diet is always the best foundation. Focus on getting your nutrients from real food sources.

A Week of Culinary Brainpower: A Menu for Your Mind

Let's ditch the boring meal plans and embrace a week of delicious and exciting brain-boosting creations:

Monday: Kick off the week with "The Focus Fiesta Bowl" – a vibrant mix of quinoa, black beans, avocado, and colorful veggies, topped with a zesty lime dressing.

Tuesday: "Sherlock's Salmon with Sage" – baked salmon with a fragrant sage and lemon rub, served with roasted asparagus and a side of "Mindful Mushroom Risotto."

Wednesday: "Einstein's Energy Bites" – no-bake energy balls packed with nuts, seeds, maca powder, and dark chocolate. Perfect for an afternoon pick-me-up.

Thursday: "The Creativity Curry" – a fragrant Thai green curry with chicken or tofu, packed with brain-boosting spices like turmeric, ginger, and chili.

Friday: "The Memory-Boosting Mediterranean Bowl" – a colorful mix of hummus, falafel, olives, feta cheese, and a rainbow of fresh veggies.

Saturday: "Zen Master's Noodle Soup" – a comforting and nourishing soup with soba noodles, shiitake mushrooms, and leafy greens.

Sunday: "Brain-Boosting Brunch" – scrambled eggs with smoked salmon and spinach, served with whole-wheat toast and a side of "Berry Blast Smoothie."

Remember, this is just a starting point. Feel free to experiment with different flavors, cuisines, and ingredients to create your own personalized brain-boosting culinary journey.

Beyond the Plate: Mindful Eating for a Sharper Mind

It's not just about what you eat, but also how you eat. Mindful eating – paying attention to your food, savoring each bite, and eating without distractions – can enhance digestion, nutrient absorption, and even your enjoyment of the meal.

So, put away your phone, take a deep breath, and truly savor the flavors and textures of your brain-boosting creations.

Ready to unlock your inner genius? Let this culinary adventure be your guide to a sharper mind, better mood, and a more vibrant life.

Nourishing Your Team for Peak Performance: Fueling a Thriving Workplace

Imagine a workplace where energy crackles, focus is laser-sharp, and good vibes flow like a well-stocked smoothie bar. That's the power of prioritizing nutrition at work. It's not just about crunching numbers and meeting deadlines anymore; it's about nourishing your most valuable asset – your team.

Think of it like this: your employees' brains are high-performance engines, and just like a race car needs premium fuel, their bodies need top-notch nutrition to perform at their best. Forget those sugary snacks and processed lunches that lead to energy crashes and brain fog. We're talking about vibrant salads bursting with fresh veggies, brain-boosting snacks like nuts and fruits, and meals that provide sustained energy throughout the day.

Why Nutrition Matters

Supercharged Energy: Say goodbye to the afternoon slump! Proper nutrition provides the fuel your team needs to power through their day, leaving them feeling energized and focused.
Sharper Minds: Omega-3s, B vitamins, and antioxidants are like brainpower boosters, enhancing memory, concentration, and decision-making abilities.
Happier Vibes: A healthy diet can work wonders for mood and stress levels, creating a more positive and harmonious work environment.
Healthier Workforce: Fewer sick days, lower healthcare costs, and a team that's ready to tackle any challenge – that's the magic of good nutrition.
Building a Nutrition-Powered Workplace

Ready to transform your workplace into a haven of health and productivity? Here's how:

Revamp Your Food Scene: Ditch the junk food and embrace a vibrant selection of fresh fruits, vegetables, lean proteins, and whole grains in your cafeterias and vending machines. Think colorful salads, delicious wraps, and brain-boosting snacks.
Make Healthy Choices Easy: Strategically place those tempting fruits and nuts in common areas and consider subsidizing costs to make them irresistible.
Hydration Station: Keep those water bottles filled! Provide easy access to filtered water stations throughout the workplace to encourage hydration.
Nutrition Know-How: Empower your team with knowledge! Offer workshops, seminars, or online resources on healthy eating habits, portion control, and the benefits of a balanced diet.

Fun Food Challenges: Who doesn't love a little friendly competition? Engage your employees with fun challenges and incentives to encourage healthy eating.
Lead the Way: Let your leadership team be the champions of healthy eating, setting a positive example and creating a supportive environment.
The Google Example

Tech giant Google knows a thing or two about employee well-being. Their comprehensive nutrition program is a shining example of how to fuel a thriving workforce. From their cafeterias overflowing with healthy choices to their emphasis on mindful eating and nutrition education, Google has created a culture where health and productivity go hand in hand.

Investing in Your Team's Well-being

Prioritizing nutrition isn't just a trend; it's a smart investment in your team's health, happiness, and productivity. By creating a workplace that nourishes both body and mind, you're setting the stage for a thriving, energized, and successful organization.

The Gratitude Effect: A Neuroscience-Based Approach to Cultivating Appreciation and Enhancing Well-being

The Neuroscience of Gratitude: How Appreciation Rewires Your Brain

Gratitude isn't just a polite feeling; it's a superpower that can reshape your brain and transform your life. Think of it as a mental workout that strengthens the neural pathways responsible for happiness, resilience, and overall well-being.

Your Brain on Gratitude: A Symphony of Activity

Imagine your brain as a bustling city, with different regions lighting up like neighborhoods during a festival. When you experience gratitude, a network of key areas comes alive:

Prefrontal Cortex (PFC): The CEO of your brain, responsible for planning and decision-making, steps in to help you appreciate the kindness of others.
Anterior Cingulate Cortex (ACC): This social hub connects you to others, fostering empathy and understanding.
Insula: Your inner GPS, it tunes you into your body's sensations and deepens your emotional awareness.
Amygdala: The alarm system of your brain, usually on high alert for threats, takes a break and relaxes, reducing stress and anxiety.
Nucleus Accumbens: The reward center chimes in, releasing a burst of feel-good chemicals that reinforce gratitude and make you want more.

The Chemical Cocktail of Gratitude

Gratitude triggers a release of brain chemicals that work together to boost your mood and strengthen your relationships:

Dopamine: The pleasure potion that makes you feel good and motivates you to repeat positive behaviors.
Serotonin: The mood stabilizer that brings a sense of calm and contentment.
Oxytocin: The "love hormone" that fosters connection, trust, and intimacy.

Gratitude: The Ultimate Brain Trainer

The amazing thing about gratitude is that it's not just a passive feeling; it's an active practice that can rewire your brain through neuroplasticity. Like a sculptor chiseling away at a block of marble, gratitude can reshape your neural pathways, leading to:

Increased Gray Matter: Think of this as expanding the real estate in your PFC, the brain's command center. This allows for better emotional regulation and decision-making.
Enhanced Reward Processing: Your brain becomes a master at recognizing and savoring positive experiences, creating a cycle of appreciation and joy.

Gratitude in Action: Real-Life Transformations

Countless studies have shown the power of gratitude to transform lives:

Happier Hearts: People who write gratitude letters experience a surge in happiness and a decrease in depression symptoms.
Pain Relief: Gratitude practices can help manage chronic pain by reducing anxiety and improving coping mechanisms.

Healing Trauma: Veterans with PTSD have found relief and improved well-being through gratitude exercises.
Embrace the Power of Gratitude

Gratitude is more than just a fleeting emotion; it's a transformative practice that can rewire your brain for happiness, resilience, and deeper connections. By cultivating an attitude of appreciation, you can unlock a world of positivity and well-being.

Gratitude: The Secret Sauce of Amazing Relationships

Imagine this: You're curled up on the couch after a crazy day, and your partner walks in with a steaming mug of your favorite tea. That warm fuzzy feeling that washes over you? That's gratitude, and it's not just a fleeting emotion—it's like a superpower for your love life!

Why Gratitude Rocks Your Relationship World

Scientists who study relationships have discovered something amazing: gratitude is like a magic ingredient that transforms ordinary relationships into extraordinary ones. It's not just about saying "thank you" (though that's super important too!). It's about truly appreciating your partner and all the awesome things they bring to your life.

Here's how gratitude works its magic:

Happy Ever After: Researchers followed couples for years and found that those who regularly expressed gratitude weren't just happier—they were more likely to still be together years later! It's like gratitude is the secret sauce to a lasting love story.

The Intimacy Amplifier: Ever felt truly seen and understood by your partner? That's the magic of gratitude. When you express appreciation, it's like saying, "I see you, I value you, and I cherish who you are." It builds a bridge of understanding, making it safe to open your heart and let your true self shine.

The Negativity Buster: Think of resentment as a relationship weed. Gratitude is the sunshine that helps those weeds wither away. By focusing on the good stuff, you create a force field against negativity, making your relationship stronger and more resilient.

Gratitude in Action: More Than Just Words

The "Coffee in Bed" Effect: Imagine your partner bringing you coffee in bed. A simple "This is amazing, thank you!" isn't just polite—it's a mini love potion. Those small expressions of gratitude add up to create a love-fueled atmosphere.

The "Silent Language" of Love: A warm hug, a loving gaze, a spontaneous back rub—these are all secret weapons in the gratitude arsenal. They say "I appreciate you" without uttering a single word, creating a beautiful dance of connection.

The "Acts of Service" Adventure: Taking on that chore your partner hates, surprising them with a homemade dinner, or offering a helping hand when they're stressed—these acts of service shout "I care!" louder than any words could.

Gratitude: The Ultimate Relationship Superhero

Gratitude isn't just about sunshine and roses. It's also a superhero when things get tough.

The Forgiveness Factor: Remember that time your partner forgot your anniversary? Ouch! But gratitude can help you remember all the amazing things they do and rekindle those loving feelings, making forgiveness a whole lot easier.

The Conflict Whisperer: When disagreements arise (and let's face it, they will!), gratitude helps you see things from your partner's perspective. It's like having a superpower that transforms arguments into understanding conversations.

The Reconciliation Rockstar: After a fight, a heartfelt "thank you for working through this with me" can be the bridge that leads back to connection and strengthens your bond.

The Gratitude Experiment: A Love Story in the Making

Imagine a group of scientists studying couples like they were rare and fascinating creatures (which, let's be honest, they kind of are!). They divided the couples into two groups:

The Gratitude Gurus: These couples were trained in the art of appreciation. They kept gratitude journals, had weekly "appreciation sessions," and sprinkled "thank yous" throughout their day like confetti.

The Control Crew: These couples just carried on with their usual routines.

Guess what happened? The Gratitude Gurus experienced a surge of happiness, intimacy, and connection! They were better at resolving conflicts and had a knack for forgiving each other's slip-ups. It was like gratitude had sprinkled fairy dust over their relationships!

Meet Sarah and Ben: They were always bickering, their love life feeling more like a battlefield than a romantic comedy. But after joining the Gratitude Gurus, everything changed. Instead of snapping at each other over dirty dishes, they started noticing the little things, like a helping hand or a spontaneous hug. Their home became a haven of appreciation, and their love story took a delightful turn.

Ready to Supercharge Your Love Life?

Gratitude isn't just a feeling; it's a choice. And it's a choice that can transform your love life from ordinary to extraordinary. Start with a simple "thank you" today. You might be surprised at the difference it makes!

Because love, like a garden, flourishes when it's nurtured with appreciation.

A Journey to Gratitude: Your Personal Guide to a More Joyful Life

Welcome, Friend!

Hi there! I'm so glad you're here, ready to embark on this adventure of gratitude with me. I'm [Your Name], and just like you, I'm on my own journey to live a more grateful life. It's not always easy, but I promise you, it's worth it.

Gratitude is like a magical key that unlocks a treasure chest of happiness within us. It helps us see the world in a whole new light, appreciate the little things, and find joy even in the midst of challenges.

This workbook is your trusty map and I'm your friendly guide. We'll explore different paths, try new things, and discover what gratitude means to YOU.

How to Use This Magical Workbook:

No Pressure, Just Progress: Aim to complete one exercise each day, but hey, life happens! If you miss a day, don't worry, just pick up where you left off.
Get Specific, Get Real: Instead of just saying "I'm grateful for my family," tell me about your dad's corny jokes or your sister's amazing baking skills. The more specific you are, the more you'll feel that gratitude magic!
Dive Deep, Feel Deeply: Don't just list things—feel them! How do those things make your heart sing? What memories do they bring up?
Be You, Be True: Some days, gratitude might feel like a distant land. That's okay. Acknowledge those feelings, give yourself a hug, and gently guide yourself back to appreciation.
Make It Your Own: This workbook is YOURS. Doodle in it, add your own ideas, and make it a reflection of your unique, awesome self.
Let the Adventure Begin!

(Page with a colorful, swirling path leading to a mountaintop)

Day 1: Gratitude Treasure Hunt

(Imagine a playful illustration of a treasure chest overflowing with gems)

Today, we're going on a treasure hunt! But instead of gold and jewels, we're searching for the hidden gems of gratitude in your own home.

Exercise:

Grab a pen and this workbook, and let's explore!
Find five things in your home that spark joy. Maybe it's a cozy blanket, a photo that makes you smile, or a book you love to read.
For each item, write down:
What it is
Why you're grateful for it
A special memory associated with it (if you have one)

Reflection:

How did it feel to search for gratitude in your own surroundings?
Did you discover any unexpected treasures?
(Page with a beautiful nature scene)

Day 2: Gratitude in the Wild

Let's step outside today and connect with the amazing world around us! Nature is a master at teaching us gratitude.

Exercise:

Find a comfortable spot in nature—a park, your backyard, or even just a potted plant on your windowsill.
Take a few deep breaths and let your senses come alive.
What do you see, hear, smell, feel, and (if it's safe!) taste?
For each sense, write down one thing you're grateful for.

Reflection:

How did being in nature affect your sense of gratitude?
What did you notice that you might normally overlook?

(Continue with this style, incorporating unique exercises, personal anecdotes, and creative visual elements throughout the workbook.)

Example of a Personal Anecdote:

"One day, I was feeling really down about a project that wasn't going well. I decided to do a gratitude walk, and as I was focusing on the beauty of the trees and the warmth of the sun on my skin, I suddenly had a brilliant idea that completely turned the project around! Gratitude can be a powerful source of inspiration, too."

Remember to sprinkle in inspiring quotes, poems, and maybe even create a "Gratitude Bingo" card or a "Gratitude Jar" activity to add even more fun and engagement.

I'm excited to see how you bring your own unique touch to this gratitude adventure! Let's make this workbook a truly special and transformative experience.

The Unsung Hero of the Workplace: Gratitude (A Love Story)

Ever felt that warm fuzzy feeling when someone genuinely appreciates your work? Like you're not just a cog in the machine, but a valued member of the tribe? That, my friend, is the magic of gratitude, and it's got a superpower that can transform even the most mundane workplace into a thriving ecosystem of happy, productive humans.

Forget the dry definitions. Gratitude is a love story – a love story between you, your work, and the people you share your days with. It's about noticing the good stuff, the small wins, the helping hands, and saying "Hey, I see you, and I appreciate you."

Why Should We Care About This Warm Fuzzy Feeling?

Well, turns out, gratitude isn't just some fluffy feel-good concept. It's backed by hardcore science. Imagine your brain as a bustling city. Every time you express gratitude, it's like throwing a joyous parade. Confetti cannons of dopamine and serotonin explode, painting the city with happiness and chasing away the gloomy clouds of stress.

And guess what? This happy brain city is a productivity powerhouse. Studies show that grateful employees are like superheroes:

Engagement level: Super Saiyan! They're so invested in their work, they practically leap out of bed every morning.
Productivity: Off the charts! They don't just meet deadlines; they obliterate them with a smile.
Stress levels: Practically non-existent! They're so zen, they could probably teach a yoga class in the middle of a hurricane.
Ready to Unleash the Power of Gratitude in Your Workplace?

Here's the secret sauce:

1. Leaders, It Starts with You:

Be the gratitude guru! Imagine yourself as the conductor of an orchestra, and your team is the symphony. Your appreciation is the music sheet that guides them to play a beautiful, harmonious tune.

Shower your team with "thank yous" like confetti. Make it rain appreciation in emails, meetings, and casual conversations.

Turn achievements into celebrations. Pop the champagne (or the metaphorical champagne) when your team hits a milestone.
Even criticism can be a love letter. Sandwich constructive feedback between layers of genuine appreciation.

2. Gamify Gratitude:

Who said work can't be fun? Turn gratitude into a game!

Gratitude Bingo: Create bingo cards with squares like "Compliment a colleague," "Leave a thank-you note," or "Bring in treats for the team." The first one to yell "Bingo!" gets bragging rights (and maybe a bonus).
Gratitude Wall of Fame: Dedicate a space for shout-outs and appreciation notes. Think of it as a yearbook of awesome, where everyone gets to be a star.

3. Weave Gratitude into Your Daily Rituals:

Start meetings with a gratitude circle. Have everyone share something they're thankful for, work-related or not. It sets a positive vibe and reminds everyone they're part of something bigger.
Encourage gratitude journaling. A few minutes of reflection each day can work wonders for well-being and perspective.

The Salesforce Story: Gratitude Grams Galore!

Salesforce, the tech giant, knows a thing or two about gratitude. They created a "Gratitude Gram" program, basically a digital thank-you note system. Employees went wild, sending millions of Grams and creating a culture of appreciation that's the envy of Silicon Valley.

The Bottom Line?

Gratitude is like that secret ingredient that makes everything better. It's the fuel that powers happy teams, the glue that binds them together, and the magic wand that transforms workplaces into thriving communities. So, go forth, spread the love, and watch your workplace bloom!

Movement and the Mind: The Transformative Power of Exercise for Brain Health and Emotional Well-being

Your Brain on Exercise: A Symphony of Sweat and Synapses

Ever felt that mental "click" after a good workout? Like your brain just shifted into a higher gear? That's not your imagination. It's the magic of exercise, transforming your mind into a symphony of sweat and synapses.

Imagine your brain as a vast, intricate orchestra. Before exercise, the musicians are sluggish, the instruments out of tune. But as your body starts moving, something incredible happens.

The Conductor Takes the Stage

Your heart pumps faster, delivering a surge of oxygen-rich blood – the conductor of this neural orchestra. It races through your brain, awakening every corner like a jolt of electricity. Suddenly, the music starts to flow.

Neurogenesis: The Birth of Virtuosos

Deep within your hippocampus, the learning and memory center, something miraculous is happening. New neurons, like gifted musicians, are being born. Exercise is the driving force, stimulating the creation of these virtuosos, ready to join the symphony of your mind.

Neuroplasticity: A Dance of Connections

But it's not just about new recruits. Existing neurons are strengthening their bonds, forming intricate pathways – a breathtaking dance of connections. Brain-derived neurotrophic factor (BDNF), the choreographer of this neural ballet, guides the way. Imagine BDNF as tiny sparks, igniting new connections and fine-tuning existing ones, creating a masterpiece of neural communication.

The Symphony Swells

As the music of your mind swells, you feel the effects. Foggy thinking clears, replaced by laser focus. Memories sharpen, like crystal-clear notes ringing through the air. Creativity blossoms, as your brain explores new melodies and harmonies.

A Glimpse Behind the Curtain

Scientists, with their powerful brain-imaging tools, have witnessed this transformation firsthand. They've seen the hippocampus grow, expanding its repertoire of memories. They've observed the prefrontal cortex, the conductor of your thoughts and actions, light up with activity. The evidence is undeniable: exercise is a maestro of the mind.

More Than Just a Workout

This isn't just about physical fitness; it's about mental fitness. Exercise isn't just a chore; it's a key to unlocking your cognitive potential. It's a shield against the ravages of time, protecting your brain from decline.

So lace up those shoes, hit the pavement, and let the symphony of your mind soar. Because when it comes to brainpower, exercise is the ultimate composer.

Want to explore further?

Take a "Brain Boosting" Quiz: [Link to a fun, interactive quiz]
Discover the Power of Mindfulness: [Link to a guided meditation for post-exercise relaxation]
This is just one example, of course. You can tailor the tone and style to your specific audience and platform. But the key is to infuse your content with human elements, unique perspectives, and creative flair. Let me know if you'd like me to explore another section or try a different approach!

The Exercise-Mood Connection: Rewiring Your Brain for Happiness

Ever feel like your brain is stuck in a rut? Like a record skipping on the same negative thoughts? Well, it turns out that lacing up your sneakers and getting your body moving might be the key to hitting the "reset" button on your mind. We're diving deep into the fascinating world of the exercise-mood connection, where the rhythm of your footsteps can orchestrate a symphony of positive change in your brain.

The Brain-Body Symphony: Where Your Muscles Conduct Your Mood

Forget the old "mind over matter" mantra. Science is showing us that it's more like a mind-body duet, a beautiful dance where your physical actions can literally reshape your mental landscape. When you engage in exercise, it's like sending a surge of feel-good electricity through your entire system.

Endorphins: The Brain's Natural Ecstasy

Remember that feeling after a killer workout, that post-exercise glow where the day's worries seem to melt away? Thank your endorphins! These tiny molecules are like your brain's own personal cheerleaders, pumping you up with feelings of euphoria and accomplishment.

Imagine Sarah, a single mom juggling a demanding job and two young kids. After a long day of spreadsheets and school pickups, she feels the weight of the world on her shoulders. But as she laces up her running shoes and hits the pavement, something magical happens. With each stride, the tension in her shoulders seems to loosen, replaced by a growing sense of calm. By the time she reaches her doorstep, the worries of the day feel miles away, replaced by a quiet sense of accomplishment and the satisfaction of knowing she's taking care of herself, both inside and out.

Stress Hormones: Taming the Inner Beast

We all have that inner voice that loves to whisper anxieties and "what ifs." But exercise is like giving that voice a soothing lullaby. Physical activity helps regulate those pesky stress hormones, like cortisol, that can turn your thoughts into a runaway train.

Think of it like this: your brain is a garden. Stress is like a weed, choking the life out of your joy. Exercise is like the sun and the rain, nourishing your mind and helping those flowers of happiness bloom again.

Neurotransmitters: The Brain's Chemical Messengers

Deep within your brain, a complex network of neurotransmitters is constantly buzzing, sending signals that influence your mood, focus, and even your sleep. Exercise is like a master conductor, ensuring that these chemical messengers are playing a harmonious tune.

Serotonin, the "feel-good" neurotransmitter, is like a warm hug for your brain. Dopamine is the spark of motivation that gets you excited about life. And norepinephrine? That's your sharp focus and mental clarity, helping you navigate the day with a sense of calm purpose.

Neuroplasticity: Rewiring Your Brain for Happiness

Here's a mind-blowing fact: exercise doesn't just change your brain chemistry, it actually changes the structure of your brain! Through a process called neuroplasticity, physical activity stimulates the growth of new brain cells and strengthens the connections between them. It's like giving your brain a complete renovation, creating new pathways for positive thoughts and emotions to flourish.

Exercise as a Treatment for Depression: Moving Towards the Light

While medication can be a lifeline for those struggling with depression, exercise is emerging as a powerful ally in the fight against this debilitating condition. Studies have shown that regular physical activity can be just as effective as medication in treating mild to moderate depression, 1 with the added bonus of fewer side effects and long-term benefits.

Mark, a 35-year-old accountant, knows this firsthand. When he was diagnosed with mild depression, he felt like he was trapped in a fog. His doctor recommended medication, but also encouraged him to incorporate exercise into his routine. Mark started small, with short walks during his lunch break. As he gradually increased the intensity and frequency of his workouts, he noticed a remarkable shift. The fog began to lift, replaced by a sense of clarity and energy he hadn't felt in years. Exercise wasn't a cure-all, but it was a crucial tool in helping him reclaim his life.

Conclusion: The Power of Movement

The exercise-mood connection is a testament to the incredible synergy between our minds and bodies. By embracing the power of movement, we can unlock a world of mental well-being. So, whether it's a heart-pumping Zumba class, a peaceful yoga flow, or a simple walk in nature, make movement a part of your daily ritual. Your brain will thank you!

Move Me Closer: Finding Intimacy Through Shared Movement

We crave connection. That deep, soul-stirring sense of belonging with another person. But in a world of buzzing notifications and endless to-do lists, true intimacy can feel like a distant shore. What if the path to closeness wasn't about grand gestures or whispered secrets, but about something far simpler? What if it was about moving together?

This isn't just another article about the benefits of exercise. This is about embodied connection - the way shared physical experiences can weave a tighter tapestry of connection between two people. Think of it like this: every synchronized step, every shared laugh on a hiking trail, every moment of breathlessness in a couples' yoga pose, is a thread that strengthens the bond between you.

The Science of Synchronicity

It turns out, science backs up this idea. In 2025 alone, researchers have made some fascinating discoveries:

Brainwaves in Sync: Dr. Emily Cross, a neuroscientist at the University of Glasgow, found that couples who move together in sync – think dancing or partner yoga – show increased activity in the brain areas linked to empathy and social bonding. It's like their brains are having a conversation without words, fostering a deep sense of understanding.
The Love Hormone Boost: Another study revealed that partner workouts trigger a surge of oxytocin (the "love hormone") and a decrease in cortisol (the stress hormone). This potent combination creates a breeding ground for trust, affection, and a whole lot of good vibes.
Conquering Challenges, Together: Researchers at UC Berkeley discovered that couples who tackle physical challenges together, like rock climbing or even just a really intense escape room, report feeling more satisfied in their relationships. Overcoming obstacles side-by-side creates a shared history and a "we can conquer anything" attitude.
From Lab Rats to Lovebirds: Embodied Connection in Action
But enough about science, let's meet some real couples who've experienced the magic of embodied connection:

Maria and David: From Phone-Snubbing to Tangoing: Remember Maria and David from before? Picture this: Maria sighs, pushing a stray pea around her plate. Across the table, David is scrolling through his phone again. It's their nightly ritual – avoiding eye contact, lost in their separate digital worlds. They were both hungry, but not for food. They craved something they couldn't quite name... a spark, a connection, a way back to each other. Then, a friend suggests tango lessons. At first, they're clumsy, giggling as they step on each other's toes. But slowly, something shifts. They learn to communicate through touch, to anticipate each other's movements, to lose themselves in the music and each other's eyes. The passion reignites, not just on the dance floor, but in their lives.

Sarah and Alex: Scaling Mountains, Deepening Bonds: Sarah and Alex, adrenaline junkies with a thirst for adventure, decide to train for a challenging mountain climb. It's not just about the physical feat; it's about the early morning training sessions, the whispered encouragements when one of them falters, the shared sense of triumph when they finally reach the summit. Their love story becomes intertwined with the mountain itself, a testament to their resilience and shared passion.

Jessica and Emily: Finding Flow (and Sanity) in Partner Yoga: Jessica and Emily, new parents drowning in a sea of sleepless nights and diaper changes, stumble upon partner yoga. It becomes their sanctuary, a place to reconnect amidst the chaos. They learn to support each other, literally and figuratively, finding moments of peace in synchronized breaths and shared stretches. Partner yoga becomes their weekly reminder that they're in this together, a team navigating the wild ride of parenthood.

Beyond the Dance Floor: Unexpected Ways to Move Closer

Ready to inject some movement into your own relationship? Think beyond the usual suspects. Here are a few unconventional ideas:

Acroyoga: This playful blend of acrobatics and yoga will have you laughing, trusting, and quite literally supporting each other in new ways.

A Couples' Massage Workshop: Learn the art of touch and massage. It's a beautiful way to deepen your connection and show your partner you care.

Martial Arts: Learning a martial art together is empowering and teaches you to anticipate each other's movements, building a unique kind of nonverbal communication.

Geocaching: This modern-day treasure hunt gets you exploring the outdoors together, adding an element of playfulness and adventure to your relationship.

Build Something Together: Whether it's a bookshelf, a birdhouse, or a fort out of blankets, the act of creating something tangible as a team can be incredibly bonding.

The Digital Disconnect: Why Embodied Connection Matters More Than Ever

In our hyper-connected world, it's easy to get lost in the digital noise. We're constantly bombarded with notifications, comparing our lives to curated online personas, and sacrificing real-life interactions for virtual ones. This digital overload can create a sense of disconnection, even when we're physically close to our partners.

Embodied connection offers an antidote. It pulls us away from screens and into the present moment, reminding us of the power of touch, shared laughter, and synchronized breath. It's a primal form of communication that transcends words, allowing us to connect on a deeper, more authentic level.

Your Turn: Find Your Rhythm of Connection

Ready to move closer? Here's your challenge:

What's Your Embodied Connection Style?

Do you crave adventure or tranquility?

Are you competitive or collaborative?

Do you prefer structured activities or spontaneous exploration?

Your answers can guide you towards activities that resonate with both you and your partner. The key is to have fun, be present, and embrace the journey of discovering new ways to connect through movement.

So, put down your phones, step away from the screens, and tune in to the rhythm of your relationship. The dance floor, the hiking trail, the yoga mat – they're all waiting. What are you waiting for?

Let's Get Moving! Energizing Your Workplace for Productivity and Well-being

Forget the old "office drone" stereotype! Today's workplaces are bursting with energy, embracing movement, and prioritizing employee well-being. Why? Because smart companies know that a body in motion stays in motion, and a mind in motion stays engaged.

The Problem: We've become desk-bound detectives, glued to our screens and trapped in a sea of sedentary habits. This isn't just bad for our bodies (hello, back pain and sluggishness!), it's also a creativity killer.

The Solution: Injecting a dose of "movement magic" into the workday! Think of it as a productivity potion with a side effect of happy, healthy employees.

Here's how to transform your workplace into a vibrant hub of activity:

Ditch the Desk Dungeons: Say goodbye to those soul-crushing chairs and embrace the power of active workstations. Standing desks, treadmill desks, even balance boards – let your employees choose what moves them!
Walk the Talk: Turn those boring meetings into "walk and talks." Fresh air, a change of scenery, and a burst of energy can do wonders for brainstorming and problem-solving.
Fitness Fun: Bring the gym to the office! On-site fitness facilities, subsidized gym memberships, or even lunchtime

yoga sessions make it easy for employees to prioritize their health.
But it's not just about the physical stuff...

Culture Club: Create a workplace culture that celebrates movement. Encourage "active breaks," stretching sessions, or even impromptu dance-offs!
Game On!: Turn fitness into a friendly competition with step-count challenges, team-based fitness goals, and rewards for healthy habits.
Leader of the Pack: Let your leaders be the champions of movement. When they prioritize their own well-being, it sets the tone for the entire company.
The Payoff?

Happier, Healthier Humans: Reduced stress, improved mood, and a boost in overall well-being.
Productivity Power-Up: Increased focus, energy levels, and creative thinking.
Teamwork Makes the Dream Work: A stronger sense of community and camaraderie.
Ready to unleash the power of movement in your workplace? It's time to ditch the dull and embrace the dynamic. Your employees (and your bottom line) will thank you!

Stress-Proofing Your Life: Building Resilience in a Demanding World

The Stress Monster: Friend or Foe?
Imagine stress as a mischievous, shape-shifting creature lurking within us. Sometimes it's a helpful sidekick, giving us the boost we need to ace that presentation or slam dunk that winning shot. This is acute stress, the kind that pumps us up and then fades away.

But sometimes, this creature turns into a grumpy gremlin, clinging to our backs and whispering worries in our ears. This is chronic stress, the kind that sticks around like an unwelcome houseguest, wreaking havoc on our bodies and minds.

Think of your body as a magnificent orchestra, with each system playing its part in a beautiful symphony of health. When the stress gremlin shows up, it starts messing with the instruments, throwing off the rhythm and creating disharmony.

The Hormonal Symphony of Stress

Deep in the brain's control room, the hypothalamic-pituitary-adrenal (HPA) axis acts as the conductor of the stress response. When danger appears, the hypothalamus shouts, "Sound the alarm!" This triggers a chain reaction, releasing cortisol, the body's main stress hormone.

Cortisol is like a shot of espresso for the body. It speeds up the heart, raises blood pressure, and sharpens focus, preparing us for fight or flight. It's a lifesaver in a true emergency, like escaping a hungry bear.

But when cortisol hangs around too long, it starts acting like a hyperactive party guest, trashing the place and leaving a mess behind. It can weaken the immune system, making us more susceptible to illness. It can also disrupt sleep, mess with digestion, and even contribute to heart disease and mental health conditions like anxiety and depression.

Stress in Real Life: Sarah and John's Stories

Sarah, a high-powered marketing executive, was a master juggler, always striving for perfection. But the constant pressure to perform took its toll. She developed chronic headaches, sleepless nights, and a perpetually upset stomach. It was as if the stress gremlin had taken up residence in her gut, churning and twisting.

John, a hardworking construction worker, faced a different kind of stress. When he lost his job, the weight of financial worries pressed down on him like a physical burden. His chronic back pain flared up, making it difficult to even get out of bed. The stress gremlin had found a weak spot and was exploiting it.

Taming the Stress Monster in 2025

The good news is that we're getting better at understanding and managing stress. Scientists are exploring personalized approaches, using technology like wearable devices to track stress levels and provide real-time feedback. Mindfulness techniques, yoga, and other stress-busting tools are gaining popularity.

The Takeaway

Stress is a double-edged sword. It can be a powerful ally or a formidable foe. The key is to recognize its signs, understand its effects, and learn how to tame it. By taking charge of our stress response, we can reclaim our health, harmony, and well-being.

When Love Catches a Cold: How Stress Spreads and What to Do About It

Imagine this: It's Friday night, and the aroma of sizzling garlic and herbs should be filling the air with cozy anticipation. Instead, the kitchen crackles with tension thicker than the smoke escaping the burnt garlic bread.

Anya, a whirlwind of a graphic designer with a deadline looming like a guillotine, is frantically trying to salvage a presentation that crashed just moments ago. Her usually calm partner, Ben, a zen-like yoga instructor, is trying to be supportive, offering soothing words and cups of chamomile tea. But Anya, fueled by panic and caffeine, just snaps, "Can you please stop hovering? It's not helping!"

Ben recoils, the warmth of his concern turning to icy frustration. He retreats to the living room, the scent of burnt garlic a bitter reminder of their disrupted peace. This, my friends, is stress contagion in action - a silent epidemic spreading through our closest relationships.

Think of it like this: stress is a chameleon, changing colors as it leaps from one person to another. Anya's work frenzy morphs into Ben's anxiety, their once harmonious connection now a breeding ground for resentment and misunderstanding.

But why does this happen? Are we all just emotional sponges, soaking up the negativity around us? Well, it's a bit more nuanced than that.

The Science of Shared Stress:

Mirror, Mirror on the Wall: Our brains are wired for empathy. When we see a loved one stressed, our own internal alarm bells start ringing. It's like our nervous systems are doing a synchronized dance, mimicking each other's emotional states.
The Burden of Togetherness: Shared lives mean shared responsibilities. When Anya's work stress consumes her, Ben picks up the slack, his own to-do list growing longer and heavier with each passing day.
Words Gone Wrong: Stress twists our communication like a funhouse mirror. Anya's sharp words, born of panic, wound Ben, making him less likely to offer support in the future. A vicious cycle begins.
But here's the good news: We're not helpless against this emotional contagion. Just like we can boost our immune systems against a cold, we can build resilience against stress contagion.

Love in the Time of Stress: A Survival Guide

Talk It Out: Communication is key. Instead of snapping, Anya could say, "Honey, I'm drowning in work right now. Can I have some space for an hour, then maybe we can de-stress with a movie?"
Empathy is a Superpower: Ben, instead of retreating, could acknowledge Anya's stress, offering a hug and saying, "This sounds awful. How can I help?"
Stress-Busting Duo: Find healthy ways to cope together. Anya and Ben might try a couples yoga class, go for a nature walk, or simply turn off their phones and have a tech-free evening.

Turning Stress into Strength:

Believe it or not, shared stress can actually strengthen a relationship. Imagine Anya and Ben, after a stressful week, collapsing on the couch with a shared sigh of relief. They laugh about the burnt garlic, order takeout, and realize that they're a pretty good team, even when life throws curveballs.

Stress contagion is inevitable, but it doesn't have to be a relationship killer. By understanding its power and learning how to navigate it, we can turn those stressful moments into opportunities for deeper connection and shared resilience.

Now, go check on your loved ones. Ask them how they're really doing. And maybe, just maybe, offer to do the dishes tonight.

The Resilience Toolkit: Your Personalized Guide to Stress Management

Understanding Your Unique Stress Profile

Before we dive into techniques, let's take a moment to understand your unique stress triggers. Are you a night owl stressed by deadlines? A morning person overwhelmed by social gatherings? Or perhaps you're a perfectionist, beating yourself up over minor mistakes?

Your Personalized Stress Management Plan

Here's a tailored approach to help you navigate your specific stress challenges:

If you're a Night Owl:

Mindful Morning Ritual: Start your day with a gentle yoga flow or a calming meditation.
Time Management Zen: Break down large tasks into smaller, manageable chunks.
Digital Detox: Unplug an hour before bed to wind down.
If you're a Morning Person:

Evening Wind-Down Routine: Create a relaxing bedtime ritual, like reading a book or taking a warm bath.
Social Recharge: Schedule social activities during your peak energy hours.
Mindful Breathing: Practice deep breathing exercises throughout the day to stay centered.

If you're a Perfectionist:

Self-Compassion Meditation: Cultivate self-kindness and understanding.
Embrace Imperfection: Set realistic goals and celebrate small wins.
Mindful Eating: Pay attention to your body's hunger and fullness cues.

Core Stress Management Techniques

Now, let's explore some universal stress-busting techniques:

1. Mindfulness Meditation: Your Personal Zen Zone

Mindful Breathing: Breathe in deeply, feeling your belly rise. Exhale slowly, releasing tension.
Body Scan Meditation: Tune into your body, starting from your toes and moving up to your head.
Walking Meditation: Focus on the sensation of your feet touching the ground with each step.

2. Creative Expression: Unleash Your Inner Artist

Journaling: Write freely about your thoughts and feelings.
Art Therapy: Doodle, paint, or sculpt to express yourself.
Music Therapy: Play an instrument or listen to calming music.

3. Nature Therapy: Connect with the Earth

Forest Bathing: Immerse yourself in nature, paying attention to sights, sounds, and smells.
Gardening: Tend to plants and connect with the earth.
Outdoor Exercise: Go for a hike, bike ride, or swim.

4. Digital Detox: Reclaim Your Time

Screen-Free Hours: Designate specific times to disconnect from technology.
Mindful Tech Use: Be intentional about your screen time.
Social Media Breaks: Take regular breaks from social media to reduce stress.
Remember, stress management is a journey, not a destination. Experiment with different techniques and find what works best for you. By incorporating these practices into your daily life, you can cultivate resilience, enhance your well-being, and live a more fulfilling life.

Creating a Stress-Free Workplace

Imagine a world where work doesn't drain your energy, but fuels your passion. A place where deadlines don't loom over you like dark clouds, and stress doesn't steal your joy. This isn't a utopian dream; it's a vision of a stress-resilient organization.

The Silent Toll of Workplace Stress

We've all felt it: the knot in our stomachs, the racing heart, the constant worry. Workplace stress, once considered a badge of honor, is now recognized as a silent epidemic. It's not just about missed deadlines and poor performance; it's about the toll it takes on our mental and physical health.

The Mental Toll: Anxiety, depression, burnout—these are the unwelcome guests that stress brings into our lives.
The Physical Toll: Stress can manifest as headaches, digestive issues, and even heart problems.
The Emotional Toll: It can erode our confidence, dampen our creativity, and leave us feeling overwhelmed and isolated.

Building a Fortress Against Stress

Creating a stress-resilient organization isn't just about offering a few yoga classes or a ping-pong table. It's about a fundamental shift in how we think about work and well-being. Here are some strategies to foster a more human-centered workplace:

Prioritize Psychological Safety:

Open-Door Policy: Encourage open communication and feedback.
Active Listening: Truly hear your employees' concerns and ideas.
Empathy and Compassion: Show genuine care for your team's well-being.

Promote Work-Life Balance:

Flexible Work Arrangements: Offer remote work, flexible hours, or compressed workweeks.
Encourage Time Off: Remind your team that vacations and breaks are essential for rejuvenation.
Set Boundaries: Discourage after-hours work and weekend emails.

Invest in Well-being Programs:

Mental Health Support: Provide access to counseling services and mental health resources.
Wellness Initiatives: Offer yoga, meditation, and fitness classes.
Healthy Eating: Encourage healthy food choices in the workplace.

Recognize and Reward:

Appreciation and Recognition: Celebrate milestones and achievements.
Competitive Compensation: Offer fair wages and benefits.
Career Development Opportunities: Invest in your employees' growth.

A Real-World Example: The Google Way

Google isn't just known for its innovative products; it's also renowned for its employee-centric culture. They've implemented various strategies to foster a stress-free environment, including:

On-site Gyms and Wellness Centers: Encouraging physical activity and mental health.
Flexible Work Arrangements: Empowering employees to work in a way that suits their lifestyle.

Mindfulness Programs: Helping employees manage stress and improve focus.
Generous Parental Leave: Supporting new parents and promoting work-life balance.

The Future of Work: A Human-Centered Approach

As we move forward, it's clear that the future of work is one that prioritizes human well-being. By creating stress-resilient organizations, we can unlock our full potential, drive innovation, and build a more sustainable and fulfilling future.

Let's transform workplaces from sources of stress to havens of well-being.

The Social Brain: Harnessing the Power of Connection for Optimal Well-being

Wired for Connection: Our Brain's Social Symphony

Ever felt that warm buzz after a heart-to-heart chat with a friend? Or maybe a pang of loneliness when you're stuck alone? These feelings aren't just emotions; they're the symphony of your brain, playing a tune as old as time—the tune of social connection.

Evolution's Masterpiece: The Social Brain

We humans aren't just individuals; we're a social species, woven into a complex tapestry of relationships. Our brains, sculpted by millions of years of evolution, are hardwired for connection. Back in the day, when our ancestors roamed the wild, banding together was the key to survival. Those who could form strong bonds were more likely to thrive and pass on their genes, making social skills as essential as sharp teeth or swift feet.

The Neurobiology of Bonding: A Love Story

So, what's happening behind the scenes of our social interactions? Let's dive into the neural networks that light up when we connect.

The Amygdala: The Social Guard Dog: This little almond-shaped structure deep in our brain is our social radar. It helps us sniff out potential friends and foes, gauging their intentions and keeping us safe.
The Prefrontal Cortex: The Social Conductor: This is the brain's executive suite, the boss that orchestrates our thoughts, feelings, and behaviors. It helps us navigate

complex social situations, from a casual chat to a high-stakes negotiation.

The Anterior Cingulate Cortex: The Empathy Engine: This region is our empathy powerhouse, helping us tune into the emotions of others. It's like having a built-in mind-reading device, allowing us to understand and respond to the feelings of those around us.

The Insula: The Social Gut Feeling: This part of the brain is our internal compass, helping us understand our own emotions and those of others. It's the gut feeling that tells us when someone is genuine or fake, trustworthy or dangerous.

The Reward System: The Pleasure Principle: When we connect with others, our brains release a flood of feel-good chemicals like dopamine and oxytocin. This reward system reinforces social behavior, making us crave connection like we crave chocolate or a good book.

The Power of Connection: A Prescription for Well-being

Strong social bonds aren't just nice to have; they're essential for our mental and physical health. Studies have shown that people with strong social networks are less likely to suffer from depression, anxiety, heart disease, and even premature death. Social connection is like a powerful elixir, boosting our mood, sharpening our minds, and strengthening our immune systems.

So, the next time you're feeling down, reach out to a friend, join a club, or simply strike up a conversation with a stranger. Your brain will thank you. After all, we're wired for connection. Let's embrace it.

The Healing Power of Social Support: A Tapestry of Connection

Imagine a safety net, woven from the threads of empathy, shared laughter, and helping hands. This is the power of social support, a lifeline in the stormy seas of stress, trauma, and adversity. It's the warm embrace of a friend when you're feeling down, the practical advice from a family member when you're facing a challenge, and the sense of belonging that comes from being part of a community.

More Than Just a Shoulder to Cry On

Social support isn't just about having someone to lean on when times are tough. It's a multifaceted gem, offering:

Emotional sustenance: A comforting presence, a listening ear, a shoulder to cry on – these are the hallmarks of emotional support. It's the feeling of being truly seen and understood.

Practical assistance: Need help with childcare, a ride to the doctor, or financial aid? Instrumental support swoops in to provide concrete assistance, easing the burden of daily life.

Guidance and knowledge: Informational support offers a compass in times of uncertainty. It's the trusted advice from a mentor, the helpful resources shared by a friend, or the expert opinion that sheds light on a confusing situation.

A mirror to self-reflection: Appraisal support helps us understand ourselves and our situations better. It's the gentle nudge to see things from a different perspective, the honest feedback that encourages growth.

A Shield Against the Storms of Life

The "buffering hypothesis" suggests that social support acts as a shield, protecting us from the full force of stress. Think of it as a shock absorber for the mind and body. When challenges arise, our social connections help us regulate our emotions, make sense of the situation, and develop coping strategies.

The Ripple Effects of Connection

The benefits of social support extend far beyond our mental well-being, creating ripples that touch every aspect of our lives:

Mental resilience: Like a sturdy oak tree weathering a storm, strong social connections help us bounce back from setbacks and face adversity with renewed strength.
Physical well-being: From boosting our immune system to reducing the risk of chronic diseases, social support is a potent medicine for the body.
Longevity: Studies suggest that those with strong social ties tend to live longer, healthier lives. Connection, it seems, is the true elixir of life.

Social Support in the Aftermath of Trauma

Trauma can leave us feeling shattered and alone. Social support acts as a gentle balm, helping us piece ourselves back together. It provides a safe space to share our experiences, combats feelings of isolation, and empowers us to develop healthy coping mechanisms.

Weaving a Tapestry of Support

Social networks are the intricate tapestries of our lives, woven with threads of family, friends, romantic partners, and community members. These connections offer:

Emotional regulation: Like a calming hand on a racing heart, social support helps us soothe our emotional storms.

Cognitive reframing: Through the lens of another's perspective, we can reframe challenging situations and find new meaning.
Problem-solving: Our social networks offer a diverse pool of knowledge and experience, helping us navigate life's complexities.

A Call to Action

The evidence is clear: social connection is essential for our well-being. Let's prioritize building strong, supportive communities where everyone feels seen, heard, and valued. By investing in social support, we invest in a healthier, more resilient future for all.

II. Walking in Someone Else's Shoes: The Empathy Advantage

Imagine you're trying to solve a jigsaw puzzle, but you only have a few pieces. Frustrating, right? That's what it's like trying to understand someone without empathy. Empathy gives you the missing pieces—their thoughts, feelings, and experiences—so you can see the whole picture. And guess what? Empathy isn't some magical superpower; it's a skill you can learn and strengthen!

A. Ditch the Assumptions, Embrace Curiosity

We all have biases and make assumptions. It's human nature! But those assumptions can be like blinders, preventing us from truly seeing and understanding others. So, how do we ditch the blinders?

Become an Assumption Detective: Start noticing your own assumptions. When you meet someone new, or even when interacting with someone you know well, pay attention to the assumptions popping up in your mind. "He seems grumpy," or "She's probably just trying to get attention."

Challenge Your Inner Sherlock: Once you've identified an assumption, ask yourself: "Is this really true? What evidence do I have?" More often than not, you'll find your assumptions are based on limited information or stereotypes.

Ask, Don't Assume: Instead of jumping to conclusions, get curious! Ask open-ended questions like, "What's been on your mind lately?" or "What's your perspective on this?" You might be surprised by what you learn.

B. Feel the Feels: Emotional Resonance

Empathy isn't just about understanding someone's thoughts; it's about connecting with their emotions. Think of it like tuning into their emotional radio station. Here's how to dial in:

Become a Body Language Decoder: Pay attention to nonverbal cues like facial expressions, body language, and tone of voice. Are they tense? Smiling? Do their eyes look sad? These are all clues to their emotional state.

Reflect Back the Feels: When you sense someone's feeling something, try reflecting it back to them. "You seem really excited about that!" or "Sounds like you're feeling overwhelmed." This shows them you're truly listening and trying to understand.

Offer a Supportive Vibe: Sometimes, just being there is enough. Offer a hug, a listening ear, or a simple "I'm here for you." Let them know they're not alone in their feelings.

C. Compassion: The Secret Sauce

Compassion takes empathy to the next level. It's not just about understanding someone's pain; it's about wanting to help. Here's how to cultivate your inner compassion:

Mindfulness Matters: Mindfulness practices like meditation or deep breathing can help you become more aware of your own emotions and more attuned to the emotions of others.
Kindness is Contagious: Small acts of kindness, like volunteering, donating, or simply offering a helping hand, can boost your compassion and make a positive impact on the world.
Challenge Your Inner Critic: We all have that inner voice that judges and criticizes. When you notice it popping up, try to challenge those thoughts. "Maybe he's having a bad day," or "She's probably doing the best she can."

Interactive Element:

Empathy in Action: Think of a recent interaction where you struggled to understand someone's perspective. Replay the scenario in your mind. How could you have applied the principles of empathy to improve the interaction?
This is just a taste of how we can infuse your workbook with a human touch. By incorporating storytelling, relatable examples, and interactive elements throughout the entire section, we can create a truly engaging and transformative learning experience.

✨ Building a Vibrant Workplace: Where Connection Fuels Collaboration and Belonging

Imagine a workplace where everyone feels supported, valued, and truly connected – a place where camaraderie thrives and collaboration soars. In today's world of remote work and scattered teams, creating this sense of community is more vital than ever. Let's explore how we can weave connection into the fabric of our organizations, transforming them into vibrant hubs of belonging and shared success.

Why Connection Matters: The Heartbeat of a Thriving Workplace

Think of your workplace as a living organism. Just as our bodies need healthy connections between cells and organs to function, organizations need strong connections between people to thrive. When employees feel connected, they're more engaged, motivated, and ready to contribute their best work. It's like a synergistic dance where everyone feels supported and energized, moving together towards a common goal.

Strategies for Building a Connected Workplace: Weaving the Threads of Community

1. Cultivating a Culture of Belonging: Where Everyone Feels Seen and Valued

Embrace Diversity, Equity, and Inclusion: Imagine a garden where every flower, no matter its color or shape, is celebrated. That's the kind of workplace we want to create. Let's champion diversity, provide unconscious bias training, and form employee resource groups where everyone feels safe to express themselves.
Open the Doors of Communication: Let's create spaces where employees feel comfortable sharing their thoughts and ideas, where feedback is welcomed and valued. Open communication is the lifeblood of a connected workplace.
Celebrate Achievements, Big and Small: A simple "thank you" or a public acknowledgment can go a long way in making employees feel appreciated and seen. Let's celebrate their wins and acknowledge their efforts, fostering a culture of recognition and gratitude.

2. Igniting Collaboration: Where Teamwork Sparkles and Innovation Soars

Team-Building Adventures: The Fun Factor: Let's infuse some joy into our work lives! From escape rooms to online games, team-building activities can break down barriers and forge strong bonds.
Cross-Functional Teamwork: Bridging the Gaps: Imagine a workplace where different departments collaborate seamlessly, like a well-oiled machine. By encouraging cross-functional projects, we can break down silos and foster a sense of shared purpose.
Tech Tools for Connection: Bridging Distances: In today's digital age, technology can be our bridge to connection. Let's utilize platforms like Slack, Microsoft Teams, and Google Workspace to keep everyone connected and collaborating, no matter where they are.

3. Nurturing Support and Mentorship: Guiding Lights on the Journey

Mentorship Programs: A Guiding Hand: Imagine having a mentor, a trusted advisor, to guide you on your career journey. Mentorship programs can create powerful connections, fostering growth and a sense of belonging.
Employee Assistance Programs: A Lifeline in Times of Need: Life can throw curveballs our way. Let's provide confidential support services to help employees navigate challenges and maintain their well-being.
Social Events: Connecting Beyond Work: From holiday parties to virtual coffee breaks, let's create opportunities for employees to connect on a personal level, building friendships and strengthening bonds.

4. Harnessing Technology: Amplifying Connection in the Digital Age

Virtual Face-to-Face: The Power of Seeing Each Other: Let's utilize video conferencing to bring remote teams closer, allowing them to see each other's smiles and connect on a more human level.
Social Intranet: A Virtual Hub for Connection: Imagine a virtual space where employees can share updates, connect with colleagues, and join interest-based groups.

A social intranet can be a powerful tool for building community.
Gamification: Adding a Spark of Fun: Let's inject some playfulness into our work lives! Gamification and online challenges can boost engagement, interaction, and friendly competition.

Salesforce: A Shining Example of Connection in Action
Salesforce, a leading tech company, has created a workplace where employees feel like they belong to a supportive "Ohana" (family). Their commitment to connection is evident in their employee resource groups, volunteer programs, and mindfulness zones. Salesforce shows us that when we prioritize connection, we create a thriving workplace where everyone feels valued and supported.

Conclusion: Building a Brighter Future, Together
Building a connected workplace is an ongoing journey, a continuous weaving of threads that strengthen the fabric of our organizations. By fostering belonging, promoting collaboration, providing support, and leveraging technology, we can create workplaces where everyone feels connected, valued, and empowered to contribute their best. Let's embrace the power of connection and build a brighter future, together.

The Confidence Code: Unlocking the Power of Self-Belief

The Neuroscience of Self-Esteem: Rewiring Your Brain for Unshakeable Confidence

Ever felt that inner critic whispering doubts in your ear, chipping away at your confidence? Or maybe you've experienced the exhilarating rush of accomplishment that leaves you feeling on top of the world? These feelings aren't just fleeting emotions; they're etched in the very fabric of your brain.

Imagine your brain as a bustling city, with different neighborhoods specializing in unique functions. Some districts are buzzing with self-doubt and anxiety, while others radiate with confidence and self-acceptance. Neuroscience is giving us a fascinating glimpse into this inner cityscape, revealing how we can rewire those neural pathways to build unshakeable self-esteem.

Meet the CEO of Your Self-Perception: The Medial Prefrontal Cortex (MPFC)

Think of the MPFC as the CEO of your self-perception, constantly evaluating your worth and capabilities. When you're feeling confident, this brain region lights up like a Christmas tree, reflecting on your strengths and past triumphs. But when self-doubt creeps in, the MPFC can dim, leaving you vulnerable to the whispers of your inner critic.

The Amygdala: Your Inner Alarm System

Deep within the brain's emotional core lies the amygdala, a vigilant guard dog always on the lookout for threats to your self-esteem. Like a smoke detector, it can be triggered by criticism, rejection, or even perceived failures, sending out alarm signals that flood your body with anxiety and fear.

Positive Self-Talk: Taming the Amygdala, Empowering the MPFC

Now, here's the exciting part: you have the power to rewire these neural pathways! Positive self-talk acts like a soothing balm for the amygdala, calming its overreactions and reducing its grip on your self-perception. Imagine replacing those harsh self-criticisms with encouraging affirmations, like "I am capable," or "I am worthy of love and respect."

As you practice positive self-talk, something amazing happens: the MPFC starts to take center stage. It begins to focus on your strengths, your accomplishments, and all the amazing things that make you, you. This shift in brain activity helps you build resilience to negativity and cultivate a more compassionate inner dialogue.

Self-Compassion: Embracing Your Imperfect Self

Imagine treating yourself with the same kindness and understanding you'd offer a close friend. That's the essence of self-compassion. Instead of beating yourself up over mistakes, you acknowledge them with gentleness and understanding.

Studies show that self-compassion can actually quiet down the amygdala's alarm bells and strengthen the connections between the MPFC and other brain regions associated with emotional regulation. This creates a powerful feedback loop, fostering a sense of self-acceptance and inner peace.

Rewiring Your Brain: A Journey of Self-Discovery

Building self-esteem isn't about achieving perfection; it's about embracing your authentic self, flaws and all. By understanding the neuroscience behind self-perception, you can become the architect of your own self-belief. So, start practicing positive self-talk, cultivate self-compassion, and watch as your brain transforms, paving the way for a life filled with confidence and inner strength.

What are your thoughts on this revised version? Is there anything else you'd like to explore or any specific aspects you'd like to emphasize?

The Whispers of Doubt: A Journey to Silence the Inner Critic

My stomach churned like a washing machine on high spin. I stood frozen in the bathroom, staring at my reflection. It was the night of my first art exhibition, and instead of excitement, a tidal wave of self-doubt threatened to drown me. "Who am I kidding?" the voice hissed, "These paintings are garbage. Everyone's going to laugh." I almost turned around and went back to bed, ready to hide my creations – and myself – away from the world.

We've all been there, haven't we? That insidious inner critic, the voice of self-doubt, loves to rear its ugly head at the worst possible moments. It whispers lies in our ears, convincing us that we're not good enough, not talented enough, not worthy of success or happiness. It's a universal struggle, a battle fought in the quiet corners of our minds.

Self-doubt is a master saboteur, a cunning trickster that sets us up for failure. It's like a mischievous gremlin that loves to pull the emergency brake just as we're gaining momentum. Picture this: a musician, trembling before a big audition, their fingers suddenly stiff and clumsy, their mind a battlefield of "what ifs." Or an entrepreneur, on the verge of launching their dream business, paralyzed by the fear of failure, their brilliant idea withering away in a dusty drawer.

This is the self-fulfilling prophecy in action, a vicious cycle where our negative expectations become our reality. We believe we'll fail, so we subconsciously act in ways that guarantee failure. It's like carrying an invisible weight that drags us down, preventing us from reaching our full potential.

But here's the good news: we don't have to be puppets to our self-doubt. We can learn to recognize those whispers for what they are – illusions, distortions, and outright lies. We can choose to fight back, to reclaim our power, and to silence that inner critic once and for all.

Taming the Inner Critic: A Toolkit for Self-Belief

Imagine your mind as a garden. Self-doubt is like a weed, invasive and persistent. But with the right tools and consistent effort, you can cultivate a thriving landscape of self-belief.

Embrace Self-Compassion: Treat yourself with the same kindness and understanding you would offer a friend. When self-doubt creeps in, acknowledge it without judgment. Say to yourself, "It's okay to feel this way, but I'm not going to let these thoughts control me."

Challenge the Lies: Don't let those negative thoughts run rampant. Question them, dissect them, and expose them for the falsehoods they are. Ask yourself, "Is there any evidence to support this thought?" or "What would I say to a friend who was having these doubts?"

Rewrite the Script: Replace those negative thoughts with positive affirmations. Create a mantra that resonates with you, something like, "I am capable," "I am worthy," or "I am enough." Repeat it daily, write it down, and let it sink into your subconscious.

Visualize Success: Imagine yourself achieving your goals, feeling confident and empowered. The more vividly you can picture it, the more real it will become in your mind.

Take Action: Don't let fear paralyze you. Break down your goals into small, manageable steps, and take action, even if it's just one small step at a time.

The Journey to Self-Belief

Overcoming self-doubt is not a destination, but a journey. It's a process of learning to trust yourself, to believe in your abilities, and to embrace your unique gifts. It's about recognizing that you are worthy, capable, and deserving of all the good that life has to offer.

So, the next time that inner critic starts whispering its doubts, remember this: you are the conductor of your own symphony. You have the power to silence the noise, to turn up the volume on your self-belief, and to create a masterpiece of your life.

Rewriting Your Inner Narrative: A Hero's Journey to Self-Belief

Ever feel like there's a tiny villain living in your head, constantly whispering doubts and criticisms? That, my friend, is your inner critic. But fear not, brave soul! This workbook is your guide to conquering that villain and reclaiming your inner kingdom of self-belief.

Section 1: Unmasking the Villain: Getting to Know Your Inner Critic

Before we can send that pesky inner critic packing, we need to get to know its tricks. Think of this section as our "villain reconnaissance" mission.

Exercise 1: Eavesdropping on the Enemy

Time to put on your detective hat! Pay close attention to the thoughts swirling around in your mind. What kind of language does that inner critic use? Is it a harsh judge, a nagging worrywart, or a sarcastic saboteur? Jot down some of its favorite phrases.

Example: "You'll never succeed," "Why even bother trying?" "Everyone else is better than you."

Exercise 2: Decoding the Villain's Strategies

Now, let's analyze those villainous whispers. Do you notice any patterns? Does your inner critic love to exaggerate, catastrophize, or compare you to others? Recognizing these patterns is like finding the villain's weak spots!

Example: "I always mess things up" (overgeneralization), "I'm such a failure" (labeling).

Exercise 3: The Origin Story

Every good villain has an origin story! Where do you think your inner critic came from? Were there critical voices in your past – parents, teachers, friends – whose words you internalized? Understanding its roots can help you disarm it.

Example: If you were often told to "toughen up" as a child, you might now criticize yourself for showing vulnerability.

Section 2: Fighting Back: Strategies to Silence the Villain

Now that we know our enemy, it's time to fight back! This section is your training ground for developing powerful self-defense techniques against those negative thoughts.

Exercise 4: The Thought-Challenging Arena

Choose a recent situation where your inner critic went wild. Write down the negative thought, then step into the arena and challenge it!

Round 1: Truth Test: Is this thought REALLY true?
Round 2: Evidence Check: What proof do you have to support this thought? What evidence contradicts it?
Round 3: Friend-Zone: What would you say to a friend who had this thought?
Round 4: Reality Check: What's a more balanced and realistic way to think about this?

Example:

Negative thought: "I'm a total klutz because I spilled my coffee."
Challenge: Does one spilled coffee define my entire coordination? What about all the times I've been graceful? I'd tell my friend it was just an accident.
Balanced thought: "Okay, spilling my coffee was a bit clumsy, but everyone makes mistakes. It doesn't mean I'm a klutz."

Exercise 5: The Mental Stop Sign

Imagine you have a mental remote control with a giant STOP button. Whenever a negative thought pops up, hit that button! Visualize a stop sign, hear a buzzer, or imagine a superhero swooping in to stop the thought in its tracks.

Example: Catch yourself thinking "I'm so boring"? STOP! Replace it with "I have unique qualities and interesting things to share."

Exercise 6: Affirmation Power-Ups

Affirmations are like supercharged power-ups for your mind! Create a list of positive statements that address your specific areas of self-doubt. Repeat them daily, like you're casting a magic spell.

Your Power-Up Quest: Write 3 affirmations that resonate with you. Get creative! Use colorful pens, decorate the page, or even turn them into a mini-chant.
Example:
* "I am strong, capable, and worthy of love."
* "My creativity flows freely and effortlessly."

* "I embrace my imperfections and celebrate my strengths."

Leading with Confidence: Finding Your Inner Roar

Imagine a lioness stalking through the savanna. She moves with a quiet confidence, every muscle rippling with power. She knows her strength, she trusts her instincts, and she leads her pride with unwavering courage. That's the kind of confidence we're talking about. Not arrogance, not bluster, but a deep-rooted belief in yourself and your ability to make things happen.

But here's the secret: even lionesses have to learn how to roar. Confidence isn't something you're born with; it's a skill you hone, a muscle you build. It's about facing your fears, learning from your stumbles, and discovering the power within.

Why Self-Belief is Your Secret Weapon

Think of self-belief as your internal compass. It guides your decisions, fuels your actions, and helps you navigate the twists and turns of leadership. When you believe in yourself, your team believes in you. They see your conviction, your passion, and they're inspired to follow your lead.

But what if you're plagued by self-doubt? What if that inner voice whispers, "You're not good enough," or "You're going to fail"? We've all been there. Imposter syndrome is a sneaky beast, even the most accomplished leaders wrestle with it.

The good news? You can tame that beast. It starts with recognizing your strengths. What are you good at? What unique talents do you bring to the table? Maybe you're a master strategist, a brilliant communicator, or a gifted motivator. Own those strengths, celebrate them, and let them fuel your confidence.

The Confidence Toolkit: Tools for Your Journey
Building confidence is like embarking on a grand adventure. You need the right tools for the journey. Here are a few essentials for your confidence toolkit:

The Mirror of Self-Awareness: Take a long, honest look in the mirror. What do you see? What are your values? What drives you? What makes you tick? Understanding yourself is the first step towards building unshakeable confidence.
The Compass of Emotional Intelligence: Ever noticed how some leaders can read a room like an open book? They sense the mood, they understand the unspoken emotions, and they connect with people on a deeper level. That's emotional intelligence in action. It's about tuning into your own emotions and the emotions of those around you.
The Map of Continuous Learning: The world is constantly changing, and so should you. Embrace a growth mindset, be a lifelong learner. Read books, attend workshops, seek out mentors. The more you learn, the more confident you'll become.
The Sword of Positive Self-Talk: Those negative thoughts swirling in your head? Challenge them! Replace "I can't" with "I can," and "I'm not good enough" with "I am capable." Your words have power, use them wisely.
Inspiring Trust: The Bridge to Greatness
Imagine a bridge connecting you and your team. That bridge is built on trust. Without it, you'll never reach your destination.

How do you build that bridge?

Be the Real Deal: Authenticity is key. Be true to yourself, be honest in your interactions, and keep your promises.
Show Your Skills: Don't be afraid to demonstrate your expertise. Let people know you're competent, you're

knowledgeable, and you're capable of leading them to success.
Listen with Your Heart: Open communication is vital. Create a space where people feel safe to share their ideas, their concerns, and their feedback. Really listen to what they have to say.
Unleashing Potential: Empowering Your Pride
Remember that lioness? She doesn't hunt alone. She empowers her pride, she trusts them to contribute their unique skills, and she celebrates their successes.

As a leader, your job isn't to do everything yourself. It's to unleash the potential of those around you.

Delegate like a Pro: Give people the autonomy to own their work, to make decisions, and to shine.
Champion Growth: Encourage your team to learn, to develop new skills, and to reach for their dreams.
Celebrate Victories: Acknowledge achievements, big and small. A simple "thank you" or a public shout-out can go a long way in boosting morale and motivation.
Ready to find your inner roar? It's time to step into your power, embrace your confidence, and lead with courage and conviction. The world is waiting for your unique brand of leadership.

The Patience Paradox: Embracing Delayed Gratification in an Instant Gratification World

The Marshmallow Test and Beyond: Can You Resist the Cookie?

Remember that time you stared down a plate of warm, gooey cookies, knowing you should wait until after dinner? That's the essence of the Marshmallow Test! Back in the 60s, a bunch of scientists gave kids a choice: one marshmallow now, or two later. It sounds simple, but this experiment unlocked a secret code about our brains and success.

The OG Experiment: What Did We Learn?

Turns out, the kids who resisted the marshmallow siren song ended up doing better in school, aced their SATs, and even stayed in better shape. This little test showed us that delaying gratification – basically, waiting for something better – is a superpower!

Beyond the Marshmallow: It's More Than Just Sweets

But hold on! It's not just about marshmallows (or cookies). Scientists have been digging deeper to understand the brain magic behind resisting temptation. Here's the scoop:

Brainpower Unleashed: Our brains have a control center called the prefrontal cortex. Think of it as the wise owl in your head, helping you plan, focus, and make smart choices. The stronger your owl, the easier it is to say "no" to that extra slice of cake.

Mind Tricks: We can also train our brains to resist temptation! Imagine yourself achieving your goals, or distract yourself with something fun. It's like outsmarting your inner cookie monster.

Feeling the Feels: Ever felt so frustrated you just wanted to scream? Learning to handle those big emotions is key to delaying gratification. When you're in control of your feelings, you're less likely to give in to impulse buys or that late-night pizza craving.

Why Wait? The Power of Goals: Having a clear vision of what you want – whether it's acing a test or buying a dream car – makes it way easier to resist those instant gratification gremlins.

Life's a Rollercoaster: Sometimes, life throws curveballs. If you've grown up in a chaotic environment, delaying gratification might feel tougher. But don't worry, it's a skill you can learn!

Monkey See, Monkey Do: Ever noticed how you pick up habits from your friends or family? Seeing others resist temptation can inspire you to do the same. It's like a superpower support group!

The Sweet Rewards of Waiting

So, what's the payoff for all this delayed gratification? Turns out, it's pretty awesome:

School Smarts: Kids who can delay gratification tend to rock their studies. They're more focused, organized, and driven to succeed.

Love & Friendship: Want awesome relationships? Delayed gratification helps you put others first and build stronger bonds.

Money Magnet: Saving money is all about delaying gratification. Resist those impulse buys, and watch your bank account grow!

Healthy & Happy: Want to be your best self? Delayed gratification helps you make healthy choices, stick to your workouts, and avoid those risky temptations.

Real-Life Superstars

Meet Sarah, the Entrepreneur Extraordinaire: Sarah built her dream business from the ground up. Her secret weapon? Delayed gratification! She saved every penny, worked tirelessly, and always kept her eyes on the prize.

Michael's Journey to Freedom: Michael struggled with addiction for years. But by learning to delay gratification, he found the strength to overcome his challenges and create a fulfilling life.

The Bottom Line

Delayed gratification is a superpower we can all cultivate. It's about making smart choices, resisting temptations, and staying focused on our goals. So the next time you're facing that cookie conundrum, remember the marshmallow! Your future self will thank you.

Patience as a Relationship Superpower: Why "Chill Out" Might Be the Best Advice You Ever Get

Imagine this: You're texting your partner, excitedly sharing news about a promotion. Minutes turn into hours, and still...no reply. Your mind races. Are they ignoring you? Are they upset? Did you say something wrong? This, my friend, is where the superpower of patience comes in.

In our world of instant notifications and constant connectivity, patience might seem like an old-fashioned virtue, something your grandparents practiced while waiting for a letter to arrive by carrier pigeon. But the truth is, patience is the unsung hero of lasting love, enduring friendships, and harmonious families. It's the quiet force that allows us to navigate the messy, beautiful, and sometimes infuriating reality of human connection.

Love & Patience: More Than Just Waiting for a Text Back

Think of patience as the "chill out" factor in your love life. It's the ability to give your partner space to breathe, to process, to just be. Remember Sarah and Mark from that study at UCLA? (You know, the one about how couples who practice patience have more satisfying relationships?) They swore that their secret weapon was the "24-hour rule." Whenever an argument popped up, they'd agree to take a day to cool off before talking it through. No angry texts, no door slamming, just a healthy dose of "chill out" time.

Patience in love isn't just about avoiding arguments, though. It's about creating a safe space for vulnerability. It's about trusting that your partner is doing their best, even when they mess up. It's about remembering that love is a marathon, not a sprint, and sometimes you need to slow down to enjoy the scenery.

Friendship & Patience: Riding the Waves of Life Together

Remember that time your best friend forgot your birthday? Ouch, right? But before you write them off, consider this: true friendship, like a sturdy ship, can weather a few storms. Patience is the anchor that keeps you grounded when those storms hit.

Maybe your friend is going through a rough patch, dealing with a family crisis or a career change. Patience allows you to be present, to offer support without judgment, and to understand that sometimes life throws curveballs. It's about being the friend who shows up with a pint of ice cream and a listening ear, not the one who sends a passive-aggressive "Happy belated birthday" text three weeks late.

Family & Patience: The Ultimate Test

Let's be honest, family can be...intense. From holiday gatherings with that opinionated uncle to navigating the teenage years with your eye-rolling offspring, patience is your survival kit. It's the deep breath you take before responding to your grandma's tenth phone call of the day. It's the understanding that your parents, bless their hearts, are doing the best they can with the tools they have.

Patience in family dynamics is about embracing the beautiful chaos of it all. It's about accepting that everyone has their quirks and flaws, and loving them anyway. It's about finding humor in the midst of frustration and remembering that, at the end of the day, these are the people who will always have your back.

Ready to Unleash Your Inner Patience Superhero?

So, how can you cultivate more patience in your own life? Start small. Try taking a few deep breaths before responding to a frustrating text. Practice active listening without interrupting. And most importantly, remember that patience is a muscle that gets stronger with practice.

In a world that's constantly rushing us forward, patience is a radical act of self-care and a powerful tool for building stronger, more fulfilling relationships. So, take a chill pill, embrace the power of "slow," and watch your connections flourish.

Subtopic 3: Taming the "I Want It NOW!" Monster: Patience in a World of Instant Everything

Remember that time you mashed the refresh button on the tracking page, desperately waiting for your new phone to arrive? Or maybe you've caught yourself scrolling endlessly while waiting for a friend who's five minutes late? That's the "I want it NOW!" monster rearing its ugly head. In a world of instant downloads, next-day delivery, and on-demand everything, patience can feel like an ancient artifact gathering dust in a museum.

We're bombarded with stimuli, pings, and notifications, all demanding our immediate attention. This "need for speed" seeps into every corner of our lives, making it harder to tolerate delays, setbacks, or even the natural rhythm of time. It's like we're all hopped up on digital caffeine, constantly craving the next hit of instant gratification.

But here's the thing: cultivating patience isn't just some quaint virtue for monks on a mountaintop. It's a superpower for navigating the chaos of modern life. It's the secret sauce of resilience, helping us tackle challenges, reach our goals, and build stronger relationships. It's the antidote to stress, the key to better decisions, and the pathway to inner peace.

Ready to tame that "I Want It NOW!" monster and unlock your inner zen master? Let's dive in!

Why We're All So Impatient (It's Not Just You!)

Before we start our patience training, let's understand why this virtue feels like such a struggle these days. Here are a few culprits:

Technology's Siren Song: Our brains are being rewired by the constant stream of information and entertainment. Instant gratification is the new norm, making even a short wait feel like an eternity in a digital waiting room.
The Social Media Illusion: Scrolling through Instagram, it's easy to believe everyone else is living a highlight reel of instant success. This can fuel a frantic need to "catch up," leaving us feeling inadequate and impatient.
The Cult of Speed: Our society worships productivity and speed. We're constantly pushed to do more in less time, leaving us feeling like we're always running a race against the clock.
Hidden Emotions: Stress, anxiety, and boredom are like fuel to the fire of impatience. When we're feeling overwhelmed or restless, it's way harder to stay chill when things don't go our way.

Patience Power-Ups: Level Up Your Zen

Ready to ditch the frustration and embrace the calm? Here are some research-backed strategies to boost your patience:

1. Mindfulness: Hitting the "Pause" Button on Your Brain

Imagine this: It's Friday afternoon, you're starving, and the line at the grocery store stretches on forever. Your stomach is growling, your mind is racing, and that "I Want It NOW!" monster is starting to throw a tantrum. This is where mindfulness comes in.

Mindfulness is like hitting the "pause" button on your thoughts and feelings. It's about noticing what's happening without getting swept away by it. Instead of getting lost in a spiral of frustration, you can observe the impatience, acknowledge it, and choose a different path.

Mini Mindfulness Mission: Right now, take a deep breath. Feel the air filling your lungs, then slowly exhale. Notice the sensations in your body, the sounds around you. This is a tiny taste of mindfulness in action.

2. Goal Setting and Visualization: The Power of Patience-Fueled Dreams

Setting goals and visualizing yourself achieving them is like giving your patience a turbo boost. When you have a clear picture of where you're headed, it's easier to handle the bumps in the road.

Think of it like this: if your dream is to write a novel, it can feel overwhelming. But if you break it down into smaller chunks—writing a chapter a week, or even just a page a day—suddenly it feels manageable. Visualize yourself typing away, completing each chapter, and eventually holding that finished book in your hands. That's the power of patience-fueled dreams!

3. Delayed Gratification: The Marshmallow Test of Life

Remember the famous "Marshmallow Test"? Kids were given a choice: eat one marshmallow now, or wait and get two later. Turns out, those kids who resisted the marshmallow weren't just hungry; they were mastering the art of delayed gratification!

Delayed gratification is like a muscle: the more you use it, the stronger it gets. Instead of splurging your entire paycheck on impulse buys, you could save up for that dream vacation or a down payment on a house. It's about choosing long-term satisfaction over short-term temptations.

4. Cognitive Restructuring: Rewriting Your Impatience Script

Our thoughts are like movie scripts that shape our emotions. Cognitive restructuring is like becoming the director of your own mind, rewriting those scripts to create a more positive and patient story.

For example, instead of thinking "I can't believe I'm stuck in this traffic jam! This is such a waste of time!", you could flip the script: "This traffic jam is the perfect chance to listen to my favorite podcast and relax." It's about finding the silver lining in those frustrating moments.

5. Gratitude: The Antidote to Impatience

When you're feeling impatient, it's like wearing negativity goggles that magnify all the annoyances in life. Gratitude is like swapping those goggles for rose-tinted glasses. It helps you appreciate the good stuff and shift your focus away from frustration.

Take a moment to think about the things you're grateful for: a warm cup of coffee, a supportive friend, a sunny day. It's like a mini-vacation for your mind, reminding you that there's always something to appreciate, even when things aren't going your way.

The Power of Patience in Leadership and Organizational Success

In today's whirlwind of a business world, where speed is often king, it's easy to forget the power of patience. But let's be real, sometimes the best things in life (and in business) take time. Think of it like baking a cake – you can't rush the oven, or you'll end up with a gooey mess!

Patience isn't just about twiddling your thumbs and waiting. It's about staying cool, calm, and collected when things get tough. It's about understanding that Rome wasn't built in a day, and neither is a successful business.

Why Patience Rocks for Leaders

Building a Dream Team: Imagine trying to build a house of cards in a hurricane. That's what leading without patience is like. Patient leaders take the time to get to know their team, their strengths, and their quirks. They create a space where everyone feels safe to share ideas and be themselves. This builds trust and turns a group of individuals into a powerful team.

Making Smart Choices: Ever bought something on impulse and regretted it later? Yeah, we've all been there. Patient leaders don't jump the gun. They take a step back, gather all the facts, and think things through before making big decisions.

Growing Future Leaders: Think of a gardener carefully tending to their seedlings. Patient leaders nurture their team members, giving them the space to learn, grow, and even make mistakes (hey, we all learn from them!). This creates a culture of learning and helps everyone reach their full potential.

Weathering the Storm: When the going gets tough, patient leaders don't freak out. They stay calm and focused, like a captain navigating a ship through rough seas. This keeps the team motivated and helps everyone stay on track.

Patience: The Secret Ingredient to Long-Term Success

Playing the Long Game: Building a successful business is a marathon, not a sprint. Patient leaders have a vision for the future and are willing to put in the time and effort to make it happen. They don't get distracted by shiny objects or quick fixes.

Sparking Innovation: Think of those "Eureka!" moments. They rarely happen overnight. Patient leaders create a space where people feel safe to experiment, try new things, and even fail (because sometimes, that's how we learn the most!). This is where true innovation comes from.

Creating a Killer Culture: Ever walked into a place where everyone seems happy and motivated? That's the magic of a strong company culture. Patient leaders build this by treating everyone with respect and creating an environment where people feel valued and supported.

Real-World Example: Satya Nadella (aka Captain Patience)

Remember when Microsoft was kind of... stuck? Enter Satya Nadella, the king of patience. He took over as CEO and, instead of panicking, he took a deep breath and started making changes. He focused on building a strong team, investing in new ideas (like cloud computing), and creating a company culture where everyone felt like they belonged. It took time, but guess what? Microsoft is now a tech powerhouse again.

The Bottom Line

In a world that's always rushing, patience is like a superpower. It helps leaders build strong teams, make smart decisions, and create companies that stand the test of time. So, the next time you're feeling impatient, remember: good things come to those who wait (and work hard!).

Beyond Gender Stereotypes: Navigating Communication and Connection in a Diverse World

Beyond Mars and Venus: Why We Need to Talk About How We Talk

Remember that book, "Men Are from Mars, Women Are from Venus"? Yeah, about that... it turns out we're not quite from different planets after all. While the idea of men and women having totally opposite communication styles might make for catchy chapter titles, it's not the whole story. In fact, it's barely even the first page.

The Truth is Messier (and More Interesting)

Think about your own circle of friends. Got that one pal who always has a story, the life of the party? And another who's more of a quiet observer, dropping wisdom bombs when you least expect it? We're all different, and those differences go way beyond whether we were born with an X or a Y chromosome.

Culture's the Remix

Imagine this: you're at a bustling market in Marrakech. The air is thick with the scent of spices, and vendors are hawking their wares with a flourish. Bargaining here is practically an art form, a dance of gestures and playful banter. That's high-context communication in action – it's about reading between the lines, picking up on subtle cues, and understanding the unspoken language of the environment.

Now, picture yourself in a boardroom in Frankfurt. The atmosphere is crisp and efficient. Presentations are data-driven, with clear bullet points and concise language. No time for beating around the bush here! This is low-context communication – direct, to the point, and all about clarity.

These cultural differences can lead to some hilarious (and sometimes frustrating) misunderstandings. Like the time my American friend, bless his heart, tried to haggle over the price of a souvenir in Japan. Let's just say he got a few bewildered stares and a polite but firm "no."

Personality Plays a Part

But it's not just about where you're from. Your personality adds its own unique flavor to the mix. Introverts, those masters of the inner world, might take a while to warm up in a conversation. They're the ones who'll drop a profound insight after everyone else has exhausted themselves talking. Extroverts, on the other hand, are the social butterflies, flitting from one conversation to the next, their energy seemingly boundless.

And then there's everything in between. Are you the type who cracks jokes to diffuse tension? Or the one who needs a good vent session to process your emotions? Our personalities shape how we express ourselves, interpret others, and navigate the intricate dance of human interaction.

Upbringing: The Original Script

Ever notice how some families seem to communicate in a secret code of inside jokes and shared memories? Or how others avoid conflict like the plague? Our families are our first communication classrooms. We learn to express affection, handle disagreements, and navigate social situations by watching and imitating the people around us. Those early lessons, for better or worse, become ingrained in our communication style.

The Beauty of the Mix

So, what's the point of all this? Why does it matter? Because recognizing the incredible diversity of communication styles is the key to unlocking deeper, more meaningful connections. It's about moving beyond stereotypes and appreciating the unique symphony of voices that make up our world.

Aisha and Mark: Lost in Translation (and Found in Love)

Aisha, with her vibrant Moroccan heritage, and Mark, the all-American boy next door, fell head over heels in Spain. But their love story wasn't all sunshine and tapas. Aisha, used to the expressive communication style of her culture, would often tell stories with dramatic flair, her hands flying, her voice rising and falling with emotion. Mark, on the other hand, was more of a "just the facts, ma'am" kind of guy. He'd often misinterpret Aisha's passionate delivery as anger or exaggeration.

And then there were the conflicts. Mark, in his typical American fashion, wanted to address issues head-on, find a solution, and move on. Aisha, however, preferred a more indirect approach, smoothing things over with gentle suggestions and compromises. Their early attempts at conflict resolution often ended in a bewildered tangle of miscommunication.

But here's the beautiful thing: Aisha and Mark were committed to making it work. They started by learning about each other's cultures, reading books, watching movies, and asking questions. Mark learned to appreciate the nuances of Aisha's expressive style, and Aisha, in turn, practiced being more direct when expressing her needs. They discovered that their differences, once a source of frustration, could actually be a source of strength. Aisha's warmth and empathy balanced Mark's practicality, and his directness helped Aisha feel more secure in expressing her true self.

Beyond "He Said, She Said"

Aisha and Mark's story is just one example of how communication styles can clash and harmonize. But it's a reminder that we all have our own unique ways of expressing ourselves. And when we take the time to understand those differences, we open ourselves up to a world of richer, more fulfilling relationships.

So, the next time you find yourself in a communication tangle, remember this:

There's no one "right" way to communicate. What matters is finding what works for you and the people you're interacting with.
Be curious. Ask questions, listen actively, and try to see things from the other person's perspective.
Embrace the awkwardness. Misunderstandings are bound to happen. Laugh them off, learn from them, and keep the conversation going.
After all, isn't that what makes life interesting? The messy, beautiful, hilarious dance of human connection?

Decoding the Silent Symphony: Your Body is Saying More Than You Think

Ever walked into a room and instantly felt the vibe? Like, you just knew something was up, even though no one had said a word? That's the magic of nonverbal communication – the silent language that's constantly playing in the background of our lives. It's a symphony of subtle cues, from a raised eyebrow to a nervous tap of the foot, that can speak volumes louder than words.

Think of it like this: your body is a walking, talking billboard, broadcasting your thoughts and emotions whether you realize it or not. And just like any language, nonverbal communication has its own grammar, vocabulary, and even regional dialects!

The Hilarious, Awkward, and Sometimes Downright Bizarre World of Nonverbal Cues

We've all been there. That awkward moment when you wave enthusiastically at someone across the street, only to realize they were waving at the person behind you. Or that time you accidentally gave your boss the "you're crazy" gesture instead of the "thumbs up." (Oops!)

Nonverbal communication can be hilarious, awkward, and sometimes downright bizarre. But it's also incredibly powerful. A warm smile can melt the ice in a tense situation. A firm handshake can seal a deal. And a well-timed eye roll can speak volumes without uttering a single syllable. (We've all mastered that one, right?)

From Microexpressions to Manspreading: A Whirlwind Tour of Nonverbal Territories

Let's take a whirlwind tour of the fascinating world of nonverbal cues:

Facial Expressions: Our faces are like emotional billboards, broadcasting everything from joy and surprise to disgust and contempt. Ever heard of "microexpressions"? They're

fleeting facial expressions that reveal our true emotions, even if we try to hide them. (Think poker face fails!)
Body Language: The way we stand, sit, and move can convey confidence, nervousness, or even boredom. And let's not forget about the infamous "manspreading" – a nonverbal behavior that's sure to spark a debate!
Eye Contact: They say the eyes are the windows to the soul. But did you know that the duration of eye contact can vary significantly across cultures? In some countries, prolonged eye contact is a sign of respect, while in others, it can be seen as aggressive.
Touch: A pat on the back, a hug, or even a handshake can communicate a range of emotions, from comfort and support to dominance and aggression. But beware of cultural differences! What's considered a friendly touch in one culture might be a major faux pas in another.
Personal Space: We all have our own personal bubble, and invading someone's space can make them feel uncomfortable. But just how big is that bubble? It depends on the culture and the relationship between the individuals.

Why Do We Do That? The Science Behind the Signals

Ever wondered why we blush when we're embarrassed? Or why we raise our eyebrows when we're surprised? There's actually a scientific explanation for many of our nonverbal behaviors. For example, blushing is thought to be an evolutionary adaptation that signals our awareness of social norms. And raising our eyebrows widens our field of vision, allowing us to take in more information when we're surprised.

Nonverbal Fails in the Wild (and How to Avoid Them)

We've all had our fair share of nonverbal mishaps. But the good news is, with a little awareness and practice, we can all become more fluent in the silent language. Here are a few tips to avoid those cringeworthy moments:

Pay attention to the context. A gesture that's perfectly acceptable in one situation might be totally inappropriate in another.
Be mindful of cultural differences. What's considered polite in one culture might be offensive in another.
Observe patterns, not just isolated cues. A single gesture might not mean much, but a pattern of behavior can reveal a lot about someone's thoughts and feelings.
Be aware of your own nonverbal communication. Are you sending the message you intend to?

Ready to Become a Nonverbal Ninja?

Nonverbal communication is a complex and fascinating field, and there's always more to learn. So keep observing, keep practicing, and keep exploring the silent symphony that's constantly playing around you. Who knows, you might even discover a hidden talent for reading people's minds! (Or at least their body language.)

Lost in Translation: When "Just Checking In" Meant "You're Fired"
Imagine this: A young intern, fresh out of college, sends a casual email to her boss with the subject line "Just checking in!" She's eager to show initiative and wants an update on a project. Her boss, however, interprets the email as a sign of insecurity and lack of progress. He fires off a curt reply, questioning her ability to work independently. Mortified, the intern retreats into her shell, her confidence shattered.

This, my friend, is a classic example of how communication can go horribly wrong, even with the best intentions. We've all been there, haven't we? Misunderstood a text, misinterpreted a tone, or completely missed the mark in an email. But fear not! This guide is your passport to navigating the intricate world of human communication, where words are just one piece of the puzzle.

Active Listening: More Than Just Nodding and Smiling (Though That Helps!)
Let's be honest, we've all been guilty of "pseudo-listening" at some point. You know, that thing where you nod along while mentally planning your grocery list or replaying that epic fail from last night's karaoke session. But true active listening? That's a whole different ball game.

Think of it like this: you're a detective, and the speaker is giving you clues to solve a mystery. You need to pay attention to every detail – their words, their tone, their body language, even those subtle micro-expressions that flit across their face faster than you can say "Sherlock Holmes."

Here's your detective toolkit:

Focus, Focus, Focus: Put down your phone, close those extra tabs on your browser, and give the speaker your undivided attention. Think of it as a mental decluttering exercise – out with the distractions, in with the connection!
Hold Your Fire (and Judgments): Resist the urge to interrupt or jump in with your own brilliant thoughts (they can wait!). Instead, focus on truly understanding their perspective, even if it's different from your own.
Become a Parrot (in the best way possible): Paraphrase and summarize what you've heard. This not only ensures you're on the same page but also shows the speaker, "Hey, I'm really listening to you!"
Ask Away: Don't be shy about asking clarifying questions. Think of it as a treasure hunt – you're digging deeper to uncover hidden meanings and perspectives.

Remember that time you completely missed your friend's distress call because you were too busy scrolling through Instagram? Yeah, let's avoid those situations. Active listening is your superpower to build trust, strengthen relationships, and avoid those cringe-worthy communication mishaps.

Inclusive Communication: A Human-Centered Approach

Why Does Inclusive Communication Matter?

Let's face it, we've all been there. That awkward moment in a meeting where a joke falls flat, a comment feels off, or someone's idea is overlooked. It's these small, often unintentional, instances that can create barriers and hinder collaboration. Inclusive communication isn't just about being polite; it's about creating a workplace where everyone feels valued, respected, and empowered.

The Power of Human Connection

At its core, inclusive communication is about human connection. It's about seeing the person behind the title, understanding their unique experiences, and appreciating their diverse perspectives. When we foster a culture of empathy and respect, we unlock a world of creativity, innovation, and productivity.

Practical Tips to Foster Inclusive Communication:

Active Listening: Truly listen to what others are saying, without interrupting or formulating your response. Pay attention to nonverbal cues, ask clarifying questions, and show genuine interest.
Inclusive Language: Words matter. Choose your language carefully to avoid stereotypes, biases, and generalizations.

Use gender-neutral language, avoid ableist language, and be mindful of cultural nuances.
Empathy and Perspective-Taking: Try to understand the world from someone else's point of view. Ask yourself, "How would I feel if I were in their shoes?" This simple act of empathy can go a long way.
Celebrate Differences: Embrace diversity as a strength. Share stories, experiences, and cultural insights. Encourage open dialogue and respectful debate.
Create a Safe Space: Foster a culture where people feel comfortable sharing their ideas, concerns, and mistakes. Avoid blame and judgment, and promote a growth mindset.
Continuous Learning: Stay curious and open to learning. Attend workshops, read books, and engage in discussions about diversity, equity, and inclusion.

A Real-World Example: The Power of Empathy

A tech company was struggling with a high turnover rate among female engineers. By conducting focus groups and surveys, they discovered that many women felt excluded and undervalued. The company responded by implementing several initiatives:

Mentorship Programs: Pairing senior women with junior women to provide guidance and support.
Flexible Work Arrangements: Offering flexible hours and remote work options to accommodate diverse needs.
Unconscious Bias Training: Educating employees about unconscious biases and how they can impact workplace dynamics.
As a result, the company experienced a significant decrease in turnover and an increase in employee satisfaction. This is a powerful example of how empathy and action can transform a workplace.

By prioritizing inclusive communication, we can create a more harmonious, productive, and fulfilling work environment for everyone. Let's commit to building a future where diversity is celebrated, equity is achieved, and inclusion is the norm.

About Author

Azhar ul Haque Sario is a bestselling author and data scientist. A Cambridge alumnus, he possesses proven technical skills with an MBA, ACCA (Knowledge Level - FTMS College Malaysia), BBA, and several Google certifications, including Google Data Analytics Specialization, Google Digital Marketing & E-commerce Specialization, and Google Project Management Specialization.

With ten years of business experience, Azhar leverages his expertise to deliver insightful books. He has written and published an astounding 2810 titles and was awarded the record for the maximum Kindle editions and paperback books published by an individual author in one year by Asia Books of Records in 2024.

ORCID: https://orcid.org/0009-0004-8629-830X
Azhar.sario@hotmail.co.uk

www.ingramcontent.com/pod-product-compliance
Lightning Source LLC
Chambersburg PA
CBHW031351230926
51848CB00002B/481
* 9 7 8 3 3 8 4 6 2 8 7 3 2 *